Please return or renew this item LEW **East Sussex** County Council
by the last date shown. You may
return items to any East Sussex
Library. You may renew books
by telephone or the internet.

0345 60 80 195 for renewals
0345 60 80 196 for enquiries

Library and Information Services
eastsussex.gov.uk/libraries

04448208

OLD AGE

OLD AGE

A BEGINNER'S GUIDE

MICHAEL KINSLEY

RIDER

London • Sydney • Auckland • Johannesburg

1 3 5 7 9 10 8 6 4 2

Rider, an imprint of Ebury Publishing,
20 Vauxhall Bridge Road,
London SW1V 2SA

Rider is part of the Penguin Random House group of companies
whose addresses can be found at global.penguinrandomhouse.com

Penguin
Random House
UK

Copyright © 2017 Michael Kinsley
Foreword copyright © 2017 by Michael Lewis

First published in Great Britain by Rider in 2017
Published in the United States by Tim Duggan Books, an imprint of the
Crown Publishing Group, a division of Random House LLC, a Penguin
Random House Company, New York. www.crownpublishing.com

Chapters in this book have previously appeared, in different forms, as: "In
Defense of Denial" (Time, December 9, 2001), "Yes, It Really Is Brain
Surgery" (Time, July 16, 2006), "Mine Is Longer Than Yours" (The New
Yorker, April 7, 2008), "The Least We Can Do" (The Atlantic, October
2010), and "Have You Lost Your Mind?" (The New Yorker, April 28, 2014).

www.penguin.co.uk

A CIP catalogue record for this book is available from the British Library

ISBN 9781846045370
Printed and bound in Great Britain by Clays Ltd, St Ives PLC

Penguin Random House is committed to a sustainable future for our
business, our readers and our planet. This book is made from
Forest Stewardship Council® certified paper.

MIX
Paper from
responsible sources
FSC® C018179

WINNING AT DEATH

There aren't a lot of living writers I'm dying to read on their own mortality. It's not that the subject lacks importance, or that there aren't lots of great living writers. It's just that it's hard to imagine even the best of them making their descent swing on the page. How much left to say can there be? Plus, you know how the story is going to end. Michael Kinsley's an exception. If it's Kinsley on the subject of his horrible decline, and inevitable demise, I'm a buyer. I'm pretty sure that I'd think that even if I didn't know him, or if he hadn't more or less given me my start in journalism, or let me in on his secret, twenty-five years ago, when he was first diagnosed with Parkinson's disease. I'd like to use the few paragraphs I have here to explain why. That is, to explain why, if you'd said to me "Mike Kinsley's just written a book using his Parkinson's disease as a window onto age and death," my mind would have skipped a happy little skip and I'd have said, "I'll bet it's funny and great and a perfect birthday gift."

The first is that Kinsley on any subject is an exception. He's always thought things no one else has thought, and noticed things that other people do not. To take a small example, he was the first to notice when Al Gore, a new, seemingly vital but self-serious thirty-eight-year-old United States senator, was "an old person's idea of a young person." He was the first to notice that when political pundits said that some politician had committed a "gaffe" what they actually meant was far more interesting. "A gaffe is when a politician tells the truth," he wrote, a line now known as Kinsley's Law. (Margaret Thatcher cited Kinsley's Law in her memoirs, seriously.) Twenty-five years of Parkinson's disease has had no discernible effect on Kinsley's X-ray vision. When he hears that billionaire Larry Ellison has spent almost five hundred million dollars on research that might render him immortal, and then sees Ellison quoted in the newspaper saying "Death has never made any sense to me," Kinsley doesn't nod his head like everyone else at the seeming importance of the billionaire's thought, and move on. He sees through to the absurd self-importance and writes, "The question is not whether death makes sense to Larry Ellison but whether Larry Ellison makes sense to death."

That's another reason Kinsley is better suited than anyone I can think of to face, at least on the page, his own death: his lack of self-importance. His awareness of his place in the universe makes the idea that he will one day have no place in it at all far more enjoyable, at least for the reader. Incredibly, he doesn't seem to be faking it: He seems genuinely to have worked out his own proportions in relation to the world around him. At the same time, he's wildly ambitious. It's an odd combination but, for literary purposes, incredibly effective. He basically wants to win at death, by writing a better book about it than anyone else, but doesn't rate at all highly the importance of his own death— which of course just makes it all the more likely to triumph over other people's.

Still, there is something here that's not quite right about this book. I got so much pleasure from it that it took me a while to put my finger on what bothered me about it. Then I realized: I can't imagine Michael Kinsley dead. I can't even imagine him with Parkinson's disease even though I've known he's had it since the early years of the first Clinton administration. He's too full of life. Too full of surprise. He's a kind of reverse Al Gore: not an old person pretending to be a young person, but a young person pretending to be an old person. I don't know that Michael Kinsley is incapable of death, or even of aging. But his book did make me wonder. As it will you.

—Michael Lewis
author of *The Big Short*

INTRODUCTION

This book is about the baby boom generation—those born between 1946 and 1964—as they enter life's last chapter. As a reasonably competitive boomer myself, I realized that the second thought of every boomer writer and journalist in the country, if they get the news of a serious or terminal illness, is going to be, I wonder if there's a book in this? Books about the experience of growing old, of getting cancer, of falling off your bike. I realized that besides the tsunami of dementia heading our way, there is going to be a tsunami of books about health issues by every boomer journalist who has any, which ultimately will be all of them. There is a lot in here about Parkinson's, because it will dominate my own experience of life's last chapter, so of course I've been giving it plenty of thought since I was diagnosed in 1993, twenty-three years ago. And you are encouraged to buy the book for any reason, including the mistaken impression that it is all about Parkinson's. The book is supposed to be funny, as well, on a subject that does not lend itself to humor. It only has a couple of outright jokes in its repertoire, neither about Parkinson's disease per se.

Here, for the record, is the only joke I know about Parkinson's. I heard it from my friend Margo Howard, who told it to me long before she knew I had the disease: Well, it seems that old Mrs. Goldberg and Mr. Murphy were in the same nursing home, and every evening they would watch TV together while she held his member. Then one day Mr. Murphy announced that he was transferring his affections to old Mrs. Meyers. Why? "She has Parkinson's disease."

If you don't get it, you'll learn something about Parkinson's by reading this book after all. Having Parkinson's is very much like growing old. The two usually arrive together, although occasionally Parkinson's strikes much earlier, or moves faster. Michael J. Fox was thirty when he learned that he had Parkinson's. As for the other diagnosis, old age: We don't need any tests. We can give that diagnosis to you right now: You've got it, it's progressive, and (unlike Parkinson's) it's invariably fatal.

This book starts with the assumption that, as age cohorts go, boomers will be remembered for being especially ambitious and competitive. Fair generalization? I'm afraid so. And even if it's not fair, the boomers are now stuck with it, just as the British Victorians are stuck with theirs. Why? There are all sorts of theories, but it probably has something to do with boomers being the largest age cohort in American history, and the most affluent. As they prepare, inevitably, to lose the game of life, which ambitions do they look back on with the most embarrassment? This book looks at four possible motivations. Which seem most pointless? Without much trouble, I conclude that it's the competition for things. Two bumper-sticker clichés more or less say it all: HE WHO DIES WITH THE MOST TOYS WINS and YOU CAN'T TAKE IT WITH YOU. The second is profoundly true, making the first profoundly wrong. Toys will do you no good when you're dead. You'd happily trade them for more time with the grandchildren, wouldn't you?

So maybe what you really want is longevity. Those extra five years would be an awfully nice gift to yourself even if your Maserati is in the shop the whole time. Or at least they would if you are mentally around to appreciate them. Millions of boomers are watching their parents die in the current American manner and saying, "No way, man. I'm not spending my last few years slobbering in some nursing home, mistaking my granddaughter for old Aunt Mary, who died in 1953." What counts is how many years you get before losing your marbles, not how many you get while still standing up. What you actually really want, or should want, is long years of good health, not long years simply breathing in and out.

Even before you're dead, you may want to ask yourself whether this is what you really want. Is being alive all that desirable if you're alive only in the technical sense? Millions of boomers are watching their parents fade until they are no longer there. As they approach their seventies, they start observing their own peer group losing its collective marbles, one at a time. And they quite reasonably conclude that the real competition should not be about longevity. It should be about cognition. Living long probably loses most of its appeal if you're one of the millions of boomers who will develop senility of one kind or another. We just don't know who among us will be the victims. We do know that in scientific studies, people suffering from other neurological conditions, such as multiple sclerosis and (gulp!) Parkinson's, are more likely to develop dementia than those in what they eerily but accurately call the control group. So the real game is cognition, isn't it? Who can keep their marbles the longest?

But wait. However well you do in the competition for the greatest toys, longest life, and healthiest brain, the best medical research indicates that eventually you're going to be dead. And you're going to stay dead for many years longer than you were alive, and all that will be left of you is people's memories of you, which is to say, your reputation. So shouldn't that— reputation—be the real subject of the last boomer competition? Aren't those who concentrate on polishing their reputations wisest in the end?

Very possibly. If you're hungry for fame, you have your work cut out for you. Very few people are remembered for long after they're in the ground. If what you want is really just a good reputation—a reputation for kindness, generosity, high principles—that should be easier to achieve (unless these fine qualities turn you into a prig).

The easiest way to shuffle off to Buffalo with a good reputation is to earn it legitimately. If you want to be remembered as a good person, then try to be a good person. Who knows? It might just work. But start now, because if you're a boomer, time is running out.

1

AN ENCOUNTER IN THE POOL

At first I thought I was alone in the pool. It was a sparkling blue gem of a pool, implausibly planted in the skyscraper canyon of downtown Los Angeles, as if David Hockney, heading toward Beverly Hills, had taken the wrong exit on the I-10 freeway. This fine pool was the consolation and only charm of the Soviet-style apartment complex where I lived so that I could walk to work at the *Los Angeles Times*. I never sleep any-more—an almost universal boomer complaint—so it was early, not even 6 A.M. I had finished my laps and was enjoying the emptiness of the pool, the faint sounds of downtown gearing up for the day, and the drama of the looming office towers. As we learned on September 11, they really can fall down on top of you. But they wouldn't on that day. I felt healthy and smug.

Then, what I had thought was a ripple in the water turned out to be—no, not a shark with John Williams

15

music hectoring from a boom box in its stomach. It was a tiny old man in a tiny black bathing suit. He was slowly, slowly completing a lap in the next lane. When, finally, he reached the side where I was resting and watching, he came up for air. He saw me, beamed, and said, "I'm ninety years old." It was clearly a boast, not a lament, so I followed his script and said, "Well, isn't that marvelous" and "You certainly don't look it" and on in that vein. He beamed some more, I beamed, and briefly we both were happy—two nearly naked strangers sharing the first little dishonesties and self-deceptions of a beautiful day in Southern California.

Perhaps sensing, correctly, some condescension in my praise, the old man then stuck out his chest and declared, "I used to be a judge." And I started to resent this intruder in my morning and my pool. Did I now have to tell him how marvelous it was that he used to be a judge? What was so fucking marvelous about it? What was his point? But even as he said this about having been a judge, a panicky realization of its absurd irrelevance seemed to pass across his face, and then a realization of its pathos. When he was a judge—if indeed he had been a judge—he had not felt the need to accost strangers and tell them that he was a judge. And then he seemed to realize that he had overplayed his hand. He had left this stranger in the pool thinking the very thought he had wanted to dispel: The old fool is past it. And finally (I imagined, observing his face) came sadness: He had bungled a simple social interchange. So it must be true: He was past it.

A few weeks after *The New Yorker* published a short article I wrote based on this anecdote about the old man in the pool—or should I man up and say two old men in the pool?—the magazine ran a response in its correspondence section that may be of some interest to people who are nicer than I am:

> The unnamed gentleman whom Michael Kinsley describes in the first paragraphs of his article on longevity was my grandfather.... Every day at 5:30 A.M., he swam in the pool at the "Soviet-style complex" in downtown Los Angeles where Kinsley encountered him one morning. My grandfather, Richard Ibañez, was in his nineties, as he told Kinsley, at that time, and had served for twenty years as a Los Angeles County Superior Court judge. If

my grandfather had seen Kinsley's article, he would
have pointed out that longevity is the wrong met-
ric by which to judge one's life. It is not the length
of life that is the "only competition that matters";
rather, it is the manner in which one lives that
should properly be used to judge one's worth. My
grandfather lived every day to the fullest because
he loved his fellow-men for all their shortcomings
as well as for their great creations. He took pride
in the length of his life not merely because of its
length but because he was passionate about life and
desired to teach others about the value of their own
lives. For his sake, I am glad that Kinsley is still in
the "competition." Sadly, my grandfather is not.
He died last November—but he swam in that pool
every morning until the last week of his life.

2

IN DEFENSE OF DENIAL

If you're going to get a serious disease—and unless
you'd prefer to die violently and young, you're probably going to—Parkinson's is not your worst choice. It
is progressive and, at the moment, incurable. But like
its victims, it tends to move slowly. It is not generally
considered fatal—meaning that there's enough time
for something else to get you first. This gives the neurologist who first diagnoses you something positive to
say. "You still have to floss" is how mine put it. The
obituaries, if you qualify for one, tend to be evasive,
saying that the person died "after a long illness" or of
"complications of Parkinson's disease." There is also
enough time for a cure to come along. And Parkinson's is fashionable these days. It's a hot disease, thanks
to celebrity sufferers like the late pope John Paul II,
Billy Graham, Janet Reno, Muhammad Ali, and of
course Michael J. Fox. Boomers have reached the age

when they are almost certain to know someone who's been diagnosed with Parkinson's. Many neurologists believe that even Hitler was a Parkinsonian (a grotesque term that makes this disease sound like a British public school or a London club).

I might not have chosen to join this old people's club at age forty-three, although you must admit it's a pretty good joke on someone who used to like being thought of as precocious. If life is a race to the finish line, I'm years ahead now. In the course of our lives, most of us will get news like this one day. And every day you don't get this kind of bad news increases the chance that you'll get it tomorrow. So get ready.

There are three ways to deal with news like this: acceptance, confrontation, or denial. Acceptance is an aspiration, not a strategy. Confrontation means putting the disease at the center of your life: learning as much as you can about it, vigorously exploring alternative therapies, campaigning for more research funds, perhaps organizing a fun run in your community. Denial, on the other hand, means letting the disease affect your day-to-day life as little as possible. In fact, it means pretending as best you can that you don't even have it.

To me, confrontation and denial seem like equally valid strategies, and the choice between them is one of personal taste. Most people mix 'n' match. But there is no question as to which approach has society's approval. Our culture celebrates aggressive victimhood. The victim—victim of almost anything—who fights back is one of the master narratives of our time, in plays and movies, on TV talk shows, in books, in politics, in lawsuits. Meanwhile, few things are more socially disapproved of than inauthenticity or a refusal to face reality. In choosing confrontation, you embrace the community (key word) of your fellow victims—another socially approved value. In choosing denial, you are guilty of self-hatred, like a gay person who's still in the closet, or a Jew or an African American putting on WASP airs or—worse—trying to pass as a white Episcopalian.

I suppose it was denial, or something like it, that led my father (long deceased) to change the family name from Krinsky to Kinsley. I have no idea why he did it, but a small part of me is glad he did. People who don't want to stand out shouldn't have to. (This rule doesn't apply to living American Jews. It's an insult to the victims of the Holocaust for Jews living in the comfort and security of America in 2016 to want to deny their identity.)

For the first ten years or so after my diagnosis, I could still pass as healthy most of the time. And even today, more than twenty years along, when my pills are firing at maximum strength I think I can bluff good health. But whenever I do, I feel a slight pang of disloyalty to the cause. A woman with multiple sclerosis once said to me, unknowingly, about disease activists in general: "We all pray for someone famous to get our disease." Although I am a very minor public figure compared with Hitler—let alone Michael J. Fox—I haven't been doing my bit.

Nevertheless, when I got the diagnosis in 1993, I chose denial. If ever you're entitled to be selfish, I thought (and still think), it's now. So I see good doctors, take my pills most of the time, and go about my business. I couldn't tell you some of the most basic things about Parkinson's and how it works. Modern culture may favor confrontation, but we are genetically hardwired, or at least I am, with a remarkable capacity for denial. It has helped, of course, that in my case the disease has moved so slowly. A neurologist called me an "outlier," meaning that I fall a long way from the statistical average. His throwaway comment made my day.

In the early stages, Parkinson's is mainly a matter of foreboding—fear of what's ahead—as opposed to any disabling or painful symptom at the moment. This makes denial an especially effective therapy. If you fool yourself skillfully enough, you can banish thoughts of the disease but retain a liberating sense of urgency. It's like having a Get Out of Jail Free card from the prison of delayed gratification. Skip the Democratic Convention to go kayaking in Alaska? Absolutely. And so what if you had no desire whatever to kayak in Alaska until faced with the prospect that someday you might not be able to? I did it a decade ago and am glad I did, because it would be too risky today. My symptoms haven't gotten that much worse, but my fear factor has grown to the point where it would no longer be fun. That's fine, actually. You need to have the courage of your cowardice. I didn't really care for kayaking in Alaska anyway. Sniff sniff. So there.

A diagnosis of Parkinson's disease is a pretty valuable warning shot from the Grim Reaper. The victims of September 11 had minutes to list their regrets. I've had twenty-three years and counting. With any luck I

MICHAEL KINSLEY

can expect decades more to scratch items off the list. Trouble is, the list keeps getting longer. But that's a different problem.

So I defend denial as a legitimate option. To work effectively, though, denial requires secrecy, and secrecy pretty much requires deception. It's simply easier to go through the day not thinking about Parkinson's disease if the people you interact with don't know you have it. This complicates the case for denial. Deceiving yourself may offend the cultural prejudice in favor of relentless self-knowledge, but it does not offend me. What you do with yourself in the privacy of your own head is nobody else's business. On the other hand, deceiving those around you is more troublesome. Especially if you're a journalist, whose whole professional value system is wrapped up in the idea of the truth—demanding it of others, telling it yourself.

For eight years, between my diagnosis and my self-outing in an essay in *Time* magazine, I was in denial. During that time I tried not to tell outright lies, but there was an undeniable effort to deceive others in order to help deceive myself. So I'm sorry about that. Some topics—*Is it decaf?*—require absolute honesty. With others—military secrets, noncontagious diseases—there may be legitimate exceptions.

The least a misfortune can do to make up for itself is to be interesting. Parkinson's disease has fulfilled that obligation. In the denial stage, it plunged me into a maze of deception and self-deception. My efforts at deception worked well enough on me, but I have no idea how well they worked on others. After I stopped the deception, a lot of people said they'd known all along. I didn't believe them. But there's no question that the levees of deception were growing weaker and a flood of truth was about to break through. There were rumors that I had AIDS or cancer. Meanwhile, the short, somewhat random list of people who knew my secret, because I told them or they'd figured it out, gradually got longer—probably too long for all the pledges of secrecy to hold.

When the diagnosis sank in, I succumbed to financial panic. Reasonably enough, I think, since PD could well mean years of severe handicap and no ability to make a living. My policy of denial was sorely tested by a brochure I picked up in a neurologist's office, aimed at people who were recently diagnosed, urging them to ignore the semicomatose lumps of humanity slumped in wheelchairs in the doctor's waiting room. Every case is different, the brochure said, and you might well not end up like this. Of course the real lesson of the brochure was that you might.

So I began "buckraking" (journalist Jacob Weisberg's colorful coinage for the world of giving speeches at conventions), which I previously had resisted. I have no ethical problem with journalists making money giving speeches on the side. It's an American tradition. I mean, Mark Twain did it! I just had never enjoyed it and hadn't needed the money. After I was diagnosed with Parkinson's, I decided that maybe I did need the money after all. So I signed up with a speakers' bureau and started giving speeches and appearing on panels of journalists whose main function besides entertainment seemed to be to add enough seriousness to these gatherings at fancy hotels to allay any suspicions by spouses and the IRS about whether they were actually business events.

Totally by coincidence, the speakers' bureau got me a gig moderating a "town hall" session at the annual meeting of the American Academy of Neurology. This turned into a regular gig for several years (by the end, the neurologists and I were so chummy that I didn't submit a bill). My role, besides introducing the speakers and posing questions, was to roam the audience with a wireless microphone trying to stir up trouble on some neurological issue (mainly, it seemed, Medicare reimbursements). This required a lot of advance homework, fast thinking, and fancy footwork, and it was a point of pride for me that I managed to fool several hundred neurologists each year.

But each year a few would come up to me after the program and start snooping around. One year Dr. Howard Hurtig, emeritus professor of neurology at the University of Pennsylvania, invited me for a drink and said, "So who's your doctor?" I named my internist, and Howard said, "No, no, I mean your other doctor." So I fessed up. And now he's a friend—just one of many I've made in the wonderful world of Parkinson's disease.

Toward the end of my eight years of denial, I had come to assume that many or even most of the people I interacted with every day actually did know my secret and were pretending not to. It was like living in that classic childhood fantasy (which was the basis for the Jim Carrey movie *The Truman Show*) that what seems like reality is actually a giant play that everyone else is performing for your benefit. Only this play has a Pirandellian twist: While people are putting on a performance for you, you are putting on a performance for them. Or are they? (And are you?) Even this orgy of mutual pretense was better than facing the truth in every interaction, I thought, and still think.

I also worried (perhaps unnecessarily, though I don't think so) about tapping too early into the vat of sympathy from friends and family. I have wonderful friends and relatives, but this thing could last decades. I didn't need that sympathy back then, and I still don't need it much, but I'm going to need it in the future. Why squander it now?

But eventually plugging holes in the dike comes to seem more trouble than it's worth. Now I've been out longer than I was in. In that *Time* essay I wrote:

The next phase will be interesting as well. Call it part two in an experiment, testing those fancy French theories about disease as a social construct. I was officially, publicly healthy. Now, with almost no objective medical change, I am officially, publicly sick. How will that change the actual effect of the disease? Without, I hope, distorting the experiment, I predict that this notion of disease as a function of attitudes about disease will turn out to be more valid than I would have suspected eight years ago.

And? Well, yes and no. Most of my friends avoid the subject completely, or they ask me how I am and then we move on. There are people who now only see the Parkinson's—like the woman at a dinner party who offered to cut my meat into pieces for me even though she had just seen me wolfing a first course with no trouble. But she meant no harm.

Those around me who knew have been able to stop acting, but my acting burden has increased. Everyone I deal with—loving friends and relatives most of all—scrutinizes me for symptoms, just as I scrutinize friends and relatives who are chronically ill. My performance, to be convincing, must be better than normal. If you're normal, or people think you are, you can clear your throat or trip on a rug or complain of a headache without raising alarms or eyebrows. When people know it is at least partly performance, you can't do that.

MICHAEL KINSLEY

Anyone who develops a chronic disease in mid-career dreads being written off—being thought of prematurely in the past tense. In 1998, five years after being diagnosed, I was offered the editorship of *The New Yorker*. I told the owner, Si Newhouse, that I had Parkinson's and invited him to change his mind, but he generously said it didn't matter. A few hours later, though, he withdrew the offer with no explanation. I chose to believe him that the Parkinson's didn't matter. To withdraw the offer for that reason would be, among other things, probably illegal. But I also doubt that he would have made the offer in the first place if he'd known.

The story ends happily. I went back to Seattle and resumed trying to create an online magazine called *Slate*. A Microsoft executive told me later that if I had taken Newhouse's offer and left the company at that early point, *Slate* would have been shut down. But now, though the Microsoft connection has been severed, *Slate* is alive and flourishing. That Microsoft executive is now my wife, Patty Stonesifer. Meanwhile, Si Newhouse got the editor he really wanted all along, David Remnick, who has done an outstanding job for almost two decades.

William Safire, the late *New York Times* columnist, used to write about a fictional character he called "the Great Mentioner," whose job it was to put people's names into circulation for jobs. All of a sudden, in Washington, everyone is saying that Senator Moron is being mentioned for secretary of state in the new president's cabinet, or that Governor Boring is being urged by leading Republicans to form an exploratory committee to consider a run for president. Who says so? Where do these names come from? Who decides who's on the list? Why, it's the Great Mentioner.

The Great Mentioner operates at a lower level as well. For a while in the 1990s, I was on the short list for all sorts of journalism jobs. After I went public with the Parkinson's, that pretty much stopped. Maybe I'd had my run. Maybe I fell off the list due to some kind of unwritten term limit under which you can only be mentioned for so long before your name begins to seem shopworn. Or maybe I became radioactive for reasons I'm unaware of or too vain to see. (You're supposed to say, "Oh, no, Mike. That can't possibly be it." Louder, please.) This is one of those things that happen to everybody in their sixties or seventies but happened to me in my fifties.

It would be ungrateful to complain about the career I've enjoyed in journalism, and I'm trying to make this point without sounding whiny: The really great jobs come at the end of a funnel. Not everyone who wants it can be Lecturer on Media Studies at the University of Southern Utah. But even if it's a job you don't want or can't take, it hurts the first time you're not even mentioned as a candidate. And that's true for Senator Moron as well. It says that in a boomer culture that celebrates youth, you no longer qualify as young. Ouch.

Embryonic stem cells are harvested from embryos so microscopically small that you literally cannot see them without a microscope. You can say that this doesn't matter—that even embryos are human beings with a right to life. But then, if you're being honest, you have to deal with what follows. The embryos used in stem cell research come from fertility clinics, which routinely produce multiple embryos for each attempted pregnancy, to improve the chances of success. The excess embryos are disposed of or, ludicrously, frozen until someone can figure out what to do with them.

Logically, if you're going to ban research using embryonic stem cells, you also have to ban the entire fertility industry, which destroys far more embryos in the normal course of business than stem cell research ever will. But political pressure to shut down fertility clinics is nonexistent.

Fortunately, scientists have figured out how to make pluripotential stem cells—stem cells that come unlabeled, as it were, and can be turned into almost any other kind of cell—out of material supplied by adults. And best of all, scientists are learning how to make stem cells out of cells harvested from the patient herself, which are less likely to be rejected. All of this is years away from actual use. No one yet knows which path is the most promising. The logical thing would be to pursue all three. But opponents of stem cell research have managed to persuade many people that the advent of adult stem cells means that stem cells from embryos are no longer necessary.

Understandably, people sometimes confuse the debate over stem cells with the earlier debate over

fetal-tissue transplantation. The idea behind fetal tis-
sues was to implant dopamine-producing tissue from
fetuses—much further along in the course of a pregnancy than the embryos used in stem cell research—
into a person with Parkinson's and hope that it would
take. The procedure requires tissue from multiple
fetuses for each patient. The idea behind stem cell
research is to develop strains of stem cells and manipu-
late them in the laboratory into cells that can replace
the missing dopamine in people with Parkinson's.
Once a line of cells that work has been developed, you
don't need more embryos at all.

Nevertheless, eight years were lost while the Bush
administration pondered the issue and ultimately
banned the research. You can't really criticize people
whose reason for opposing research that uses embryos
is that they truly believe embryos are fully human beings. But you can criticize politicians who try to escape
this yes-or-no dilemma with calls for compromise or
delay or prestigious panels to study the situation and
report back in a few months. Can't they hear that
sound of clocks ticking? *Tempus fugit,* assholes.

The news is more interesting when your life may

depend on it. I used to skip the Science section of the *New York Times*. No more. So that's another little plus of having Parkinson's disease. I don't delude myself that the pluses add up to equal the minuses. Though I may give that a try.

3

IT'S NOT ROCKET SCIENCE—
BUT IT IS BRAIN SURGERY

Like NASA before the first moon landing, I devoted a lot of time and energy to thinking about what to say when I woke up from brain surgery. That's right, brain surgery—it's a real conversation stopper, isn't it? There aren't many things you can say these days that retain their shock value, but that is one of them. "So, Mike, got any summer plans?" "Why, yes, next Tuesday I'm having brain surgery. How about you?" In the age of angioplasty and Lipitor, even the heart has lost much of its metaphorical power, at least in the medical context. People are willing to accept it as a collection of muscles and blood vessels rather than—or at least in addition to—the seat of various emotions. But the brain remains the seat of the self itself, in physical reality as well as in metaphor. And the brain as metaphor looms so large that there isn't much room left for the simultaneous physical reality that the brain is material, performs mechanical functions, can break down, and sometimes can be repaired. So brain surgery remains shocking and mystical. People don't expect to run into someone who's having brain surgery next week squeezing the melons at Whole Foods. (Unless, of course, he's squeezing them and shrieking, "Why don't you answer? Hello? Hello?")

Self-indulgently, in the weeks before my surgery, I dropped the conversational bomb of brain surgery more often than absolutely necessary, just to enjoy the reaction. And why not? I deserved that treat. After all, I was going to be having brain surgery.

Brain surgery is a license for self-indulgence. Cancel that dentist's appointment; you've suffered enough. (Though technically, before you go under, you haven't actually suffered at all.) Every activity, large or small, routine or special, takes on an epic quality. Take out the trash? "C'mon, honey, I've got BRAIN SURGERY next week."

Writers devote a lot of creative energy to dreaming up reasons not to write. One of the all-time best came a few years ago from my friend Anne Applebaum, the foreign affairs columnist, who told her readers that she was going to stop writing her column for a while because her husband had become defense minister of Poland and she was moving to Warsaw. Sure, Anne, and I'm taking the summer off because I'm having brain surgery. In Cleveland. But it was true. The operation is called deep brain stimulation (DBS). They stick a couple of wires into your head, run them around your ears and into batteries that are implanted in your chest. Then current from the batteries zaps some bad signals in your brain so that good signals can be heard by the rest of your body. Or something like that. When it works, as it generally does, it greatly reduces the symptoms of Parkinson's disease.

I had the operation in 2006 at the Cleveland Clinic. Back then the operation was approved by the Food and Drug Administration, and therefore no longer classified as "experimental," but it was not yet widely available. By now, no respectable medical center (what used to be called a hospital) would be caught dead without one.

You may have guessed, from the existence of the book you hold in your hands, that the surgery went well. And thank you for your concern. Now, where was I? Oh, yes, brain surgery. Thinking I would give self-deception one more shot, I tried to convince myself in the days leading up to the operation that DBS isn't really brain surgery. They don't crack open your skull; they just drill a couple of small holes to put the wires through. Tiny holes. Itsy-bitsy holes. Teensy-weensy little holes. Yet the propaganda they give you when you sign up for the operation describes the holes as "dime-sized." That took me aback. The dime, there's no denying, is a seriously undersized coin. But frankly, I hadn't been thinking coins at all. I'd been thinking grains of sand. A dime is huge! The hospital printout of all the things you can't do afterward describes DBS as "major brain surgery." Is there such a thing as minor brain surgery? Not now, maybe, but in the future. Dr. Ali Rezai is endlessly enthusiastic about the potential of stem cells. He predicts DBS will be a forty-five-minute office visit rather than the nine-hour ordeal I endured.

To an American middle-class professional of the twenty-first century, what is scariest about brain surgery isn't the ever-present risk of disaster or even the chance of unexpected side effects. It's the danger that people will look at you differently. We are all brain snobs, and we are all—those of us over twenty or so—losing brain cells. But if you're walking around with wires in your head and batteries flanking your chest, every senior moment when you can't remember the term for, you know, when they drill holes in your skull—right, brain surgery—is . . . is . . . is . . . well, it's going to seem significant to others and to you.

That's why my first words coming out of surgery were so important. They had to show the world—and convince me—that I was all there. Of course, there are the obvious jokes about brain surgery ("Well, it wasn't exactly rocket science"). There is Dada ("I am the defense minister of Poland. Who the hell are you?"). And slapstick ("I feel as if I've lost ten pounds . . . uh-oh"). I did lots of thinking about this, and here's what I ultimately came up with: "Well, of course. When you cut taxes, government revenues go up. Why couldn't I see that before?"

4

AN ENCOUNTER IN THE SKY

On an airplane long ago—fifteen or twenty years—I turned and discovered Robert McNamara in the next seat. McNamara needs no introduction for people over, say, sixty but—shockingly—probably does for most of the American population. Robert Strange McNamara, I should therefore explain for anyone middle-aged or younger, was secretary of defense for seven years under Presidents John F. Kennedy and Lyndon Johnson. He must have been in his early eighties at the time of our encounter.

McNamara was an architect of the Vietnam War, which remains the defining experience of my generation, for those who served in it as well as those who protested against it, along with those who only listened to the music. The year was 1975 when the helicopters took off from the roof of the American embassy in Saigon, bearing the last Americans; a few of the embassy staff and others who had been loyal to us to the end (and who therefore thought it would be unwise to hang around); and miscellaneous Vietnamese, desperate to get out for a variety of good reasons. The years since have hardly been boring. And maybe AIDS, Iraq, 9/11, and whatever else fate has lined up to keep us amused will make Vietnam seem small in hindsight. But I doubt it, don't you? And I don't think that's just generational vanity.

McNamara himself turned against the war—though never publicly or explicitly—and resigned as defense secretary in 1968 to become head of the World Bank. Our plane was going to Denver, and I asked him what was taking him there. He said that he was meeting a female friend at the Denver airport and then heading for Aspen. It seems that when his wife died he had sponsored in her memory one of a chain of primitive huts on a cross-country ski trail between Aspen and Vail. Now he was going to ski the trail and stay in the huts with his lady friend. He told me this, then beamed, like my pal the judge in the pool.

Well, life is unfair, but let's not get carried away.

Longevity is not a zero-sum game. A longer life for Robert McNamara doesn't mean a shorter life for you or me or the average citizen of Vietnam. He did that damage long ago, and won't be doing any more. In fact, he seems to have spent the gift of a long life trying to make amends—mainly, as he described his recent agenda to me, by flying around the world to conferences where the world's suffering is deplored. Nevertheless.

To get to that view of things, though, I had to suppress an irrational feeling that McNamara had won big in a game he shouldn't have been. Yes, life is unfair, and never more so than in how much of itself it gives to different people. Deaths of children and young adults are mourned with special pain, and the very, very old are celebrated. But death at any age between about sixty and about ninety doesn't rate a second glance as you flip through the obituaries. (Oh yes, you do.) Death anywhere between sixty and ninety is considered a "normal" life span, even though the ninety-year-old got 50 percent more life than the sixty-year-old.

What's more, of all the gifts that life and luck can bestow—money, good looks, love, power—longevity is the one that people seem least reluctant to brag about. In fact, they routinely claim it as some sort of virtue—as if living to ninety were primarily the result of hard work or prayer, rather than good genes and never getting run over by a truck. Maybe the possibility that the truck is on your agenda for later this morning makes the bragging acceptable. The longevity game is one that really isn't over till it's over.

Between what your parents gave you to start with—genetically or culturally or financially—and pure luck, you play a small role in determining how long you live. And even if you add a few years through your own initiative, by doing all the right things in terms of diet, exercise, sleep, vitamins, and so on, why is that to your moral credit? Extending your own life expectancy is the most selfish motive imaginable for doing anything. Do it, by all means. I do. But for heaven's sake, don't take a bow and expect applause.

This is the game that really counts. Perhaps you imagine that, as eternity approaches, the petty ambitions and rivalries of this life melt away. Perhaps they do. That doesn't mean that the competition is over. It means that the biggest competition of all is about to start. Do you doubt it? Ask yourself: what do you have now, and what do you covet, that you would not gladly trade for, say, five extra years? These would be good years, of cross-country skiing between fashionable Colorado resorts, or at least years when you could still walk and think and read. You would still be a player in whatever game you spent your life playing: still invited to faraway conferences about other people's problems, if you ever were; still baking your famous chocolate chip banana bread for the family, if your life followed a less McNamarish course. What would you trade for that? Or, rather, what wouldn't you trade? Okay, you'd give up years for the health and happiness of your children. What else? Peace in the Middle East? A solution to global warming? A cure for AIDS? These negotiations are secret, mind you. No one will know if you selfishly choose a few extra years for yourself over an extra million or two for planet Earth. We'll posit that you're a good person, though, and that to spare the earth from a couple of the Four Horsemen, you'd accept a shorter span for yourself.

Few people ever have the opportunity to make an explicit choice between extra years of life for themselves and some noble cause or other. Among those who do are soldiers. People who volunteer for military service or act bravely in battle consciously risk giving up most of their biblically allotted three score and ten, and for some who do, this choice is both wise and generous beyond belief. Unfortunately, every war has at least two sides, and at most one of them is the good side. The math suggests that, in the course of history, most of these sacrifices probably were a mistake. Robert McNamara's years were enough to equal the life spans of four soldiers who died in Vietnam.

Anyway, enough about Robert McNamara. Back to you. Children, country, future of the world, are off the table. And, yes, these are the important things. But there are also other, less exalted things that make life sweet. The baby boom generation in America is thought to have found something approaching genuine happiness in material possessions. Remember that bumper sticker HE WHO DIES WITH THE MOST TOYS WINS? This was thought to be a mordant encapsulation of the baby boom generation's shallowness, greed, excessive competitiveness, and love of possessions. And it may well be all of these things. It's also fundamentally wrong. Is there anything in the Hammacher Schlemmer catalogue—or even listed on realtor.com—for which you would give up five years?

Of course not. That sports car may be to die for, but in fact you wouldn't. Die for it, that is. What good are the toys if you're dead? "He who dies last"—he's the one who wins.

Competitive consumerism wasn't invented by boomers, or yuppies, as they're sometimes called. What's the difference between a boomer and a yuppie? (Sounds like we're building up to a punch line here, but there's no joke. Sorry.) Boomers—short for baby boomers—are Americans born during the "baby boom" that followed the end of World War II, as millions of couples tried to make up for lost time. Boomers include everybody born in the years between 1946—the earliest date at which a serviceman returning from Europe after the war could come home and join his wife in producing a baby—and 1964, the last year anyone could reasonably use celebration of the Allied victory in World War II as a reason for having sex.

Yuppies—short for "young urban professionals"—refers to a subset of boomers: the trendsetters who moved from the suburbs where they grew up into tastefully restored town houses in the inner cities. The ones who first discovered Starbucks (and were the first to reject it and move on to espresso machines). The ones who—well, you know who you are. All boomers aren't yuppies, but almost all boomers have been heavily influenced by yuppies in their lifestyle choices. In fact, the very notion of a "lifestyle"—that all the major aspects of your life (your work, your family, your clothes, your spiritual beliefs, your kitchen equipment) should be conscious decisions, or really one big conscious decision about the shape of your life—is a core yuppie value widely adopted not just by boomers but by the nation at large.

Boomers realize the ultimate folly of competitive consumerism, of course. Don't forget: Back in the Dark Ages, we invented jogging. More important, we invented the jogging shoe: a whole industry aimed right at the boomer sweet spot. Our knees now regret it—too late, too late. A new malady was also invented to go along with the jogging shoes. That is the dreaded "pronation." It's been a remarkable development. No one in America was known to suffer from pronation until around 1965. Now, pronation is tied with knee problems and back problems at number 17 on *Esquire*'s annual list of the top conversational topics to avoid. (The inventor and master of these shopping lists as commentary on lost time is David Brooks of the *New York Times,* who really deserves credit, if not actual royalties, for them. Fortunately for me, one of the themes of this book is that few people get what they deserve, in this life or the next one.)

The passion for Things and the hunger to acquire them are deeply rooted in yuppie culture. I win if my house is bigger than yours, or if my cell phone is smaller. Or if my laptop computer is thinner or my hiking boots are thicker. And yet all this is meaningless, isn't it? And I don't mean that in a spiritual or moral way. Be as greedy and self-centered as you want. The only competition that matters, in the end, is about life itself. And the standard is clear: "Mine is longer than yours."

The oldest boomers, born in the late 1940s, are approaching seventy. Seventy! This surely was not supposed to happen. But it has happened. The early heats of the Boomer Games are already over, and they stop, mercifully, at around eighty, where the first boomers will start to arrive in 2026. Welcome to the age of competitive longevity.

So how are you doing? Let's say you're sixty-five. To begin with, you're still alive, which gives you a leg up.

Or are the real winners in our youth-obsessed genera-tion the boomers who died young, like John Belushi and Janis Joplin? Well, perhaps, but you've already missed that boat. There may be glamour in dying in your early twenties. There is no glamour in dying in your late fifties.

The *Washington Post* carried an amusing article a while ago about tech billionaires facing the very real problem of what to do with their money once they've bought every imaginable toy up to and including the private plane and yet still have billions left. There is the Bill Gates model: They can use the money for good works. All of them do some of that—it's hard to avoid. But at some point the logic of "mine is longer than yours" reasserts itself and you decide to spend some money trying to live forever.

The leading immortophiliac is Larry Ellison, the longtime CEO of Oracle. At the time the article was published, in April 2015, Ellison had invested more than $430 million in antiaging research. The article quotes Ellison from a book about him: "Death has never made any sense to me. How can a person be there and then just vanish, just not be there?" Actu-ally the question is not whether death makes sense to

Larry Ellison but whether Larry Ellison makes sense to death. And I'm afraid he does.

For someone born in the United States in 2013, the most recent year for which there are final figures, life expectancy is 78.8 years. That's 76.4 years for males and 81.2 years for females. But if you've made it to 65, your life expectancy is 82.9 if you're a man and 85.5 if you're a woman. (In Katha Pollitt's book of essays *Learning to Drive,* there is a vicious one called "After the Men Are Dead.") The mortality tables are fun to play with, in a ghoulish way. The United States comes in a shameful fifty-third, behind Ireland, Bosnia, and Bermuda, among other countries. It's not true, however, as you often hear, that they do better in Cuba than we do. Our life expectancy in the United States is 0.49 years longer than Cuba's. And before you laugh off 0.49 years, consider that 0.49 years is just under 6 months: one last golden spring and summer with the grandchildren. How much is that worth to you?

Ellison's quest for eternal life is likely to be disappointing. But I have an idea for him. He should redefine his goal slightly and consider the project a success if it merely achieves a measurable increase in life expectancy and not actual immortality. In fact, he's in luck because half a billion dollars could extend the lives of many thousands, if not millions, of people if spent on such things as mosquito nets to fight malaria rather than exotic cancer treatments for people such as Larry Ellison. This has been the approach of the Bill and Melinda Gates Foundation, which has added more life-years to the planet simply by bringing the underdeveloped world a small step toward the standards of the Western world than any amount of money will ever achieve by keeping Larry Ellison alive until he turns 100 in 28 years. (My wife is former CEO of the Gates Foundation, so I may be biased here.) On the other hand, I am the beneficiary of high-tech medicine, specifically deep brain stimulation for Parkinson's. So I have mixed feelings.

But enough about Larry Ellison. Back to you. Of course, all these life-expectancy figures are only averages. Factors that you control, such as diet, exercise, and smoking, can affect your score. So can factors that are beyond your control but are already known or knowable, such as your family health history. What most affects your own outcome, though, is the simple fact that averages are only averages. Think of this as good news: In order for the averages to work out, for every person who dies in his forties, there must be three or four who make it into their eighties.

You might compare the boomer longevity competition to a tontine. This was a macabre form of investment, popular in Europe and America in the seventeenth, eighteenth, and nineteenth centuries. In its simplest form, a group of investors would each put a certain amount of money into a pool, and the money would sit there accumulating interest until all but one of the members had died, then that one survivor would get the whole pile. There's a very funny movie about a tontine called *The Wrong Box* starring Michael Caine. A tontine is the ultimate in "moral hazard," an insurance industry term for the temptation to cause whatever it is you are insuring yourself against. For example, fire insurance encouraging fires. Or a tontine encouraging people to murder one another.

(Old moral-hazard joke: Three elderly retirees are sitting on the beach in Florida. One of them asks the other two, "What brought you here?" Second guy says, "I had a small factory up north, but it burned down in a mysterious fire. So I took the insurance money and retired to Florida." Third guy says, "Me too. Owned a factory. Mysterious fire. Insurance money. Florida."

He turns to the first guy. "And how about you?" First guy says, "Same story, almost. My factory was wiped out in a huge tidal wave, so I took the insurance money and moved to Florida." The other two look at each other, and finally one says, "Gosh, who do you go to for a tidal wave?")

A tontine sounds like the kind of thing we don't have anymore, but in fact the Social Security system is sort of like a tontine: We all put in the same fraction of our wages (with ceilings and other complications). And because you get a check every month, the amount you get back depends on how long you live. Social Security is insurance against longevity. Except that longevity is something we all want. So people who die young are doubly screwed. First, they lose those years, and second, they lose Social Security benefits.

African Americans on average live over three years less than the white population. So they are among the double losers. Women, who live longer than men, are double winners. It's hard to think what, if anything, can be done about this. By its nature, insurance is a pooling of risks. If we could all pay in or draw out from Social Security according to our own risk profile, there would still be winners and losers, people who do dramatically better or worse (live longer or die earlier) than their profiles would predict.

And actually life itself is sort of like a tontine. The winners are the ones who outlive their friends. Even without a cash prize, we all would like to win. Life would be pretty empty without your friends. But not as empty as death.

We are born thinking that we'll live forever. Then death becomes an intermittent reality, as grandparents and parents die, and tragedy of some kind removes one or two from our own age cohort. And then, at some point, death becomes a normal part of life—a faint dirge in the background that gradually gets louder. What is that point? One crude measure would be when you can expect, on average, one person of roughly your age in your family or social circle to die every year. At that point, any given death can still be a terrible and unexpected blow, but the fact that people your age die is no longer a legitimate surprise, and the related fact that you will die, too, is no longer avoidable.

With some heroic assumptions, we can come up with an age when death starts to be in-your-face. We will merge all sexual and racial categories into a single composite American. We will assume that there are

100 people your age who are close enough to be invited to your funeral. Your funeral chapel won't fit 100 people? No problem. On average, half of them will be too busy decomposing to attend. As Max Beerbohm noted in his novel, *Zuleika Dobson,* "Death cancels all engagements." And why 100? Because it's easy, and also because it's two-thirds of "Dunbar's number," of 150, which is supposedly the most relationships that any one set of human neurons can handle. We're crudely assuming that two-thirds of those are about your age.

Anyway, the answer is age 63. If a hundred Americans start the voyage of life together, on average one of them will have died by the time the group turns 16. At 40, their lives are half over: Further life expectancy at age 40 is 39.9. And at age 63, the group starts losing an average of one person every year. Then it accelerates. By age 75, sixty-seven of the original one hundred are left. By age 100, three remain.

The last boomer competition is not just about how long you live. It is also about how you die. This one is a "Mine is shorter than yours": You want a death that is painless and quick. Even here there are choices. What is "quick"? You might prefer something instantaneous, like walking down Fifth Avenue and being hit by a flowerpot that falls off an upper-story windowsill. Or, if you're the orderly type, you might prefer a brisk but not sudden slide into oblivion. Take a couple of months, pain-free but weakening in some vague nineteenth-century way. You can use the time to make your farewells, plan your funeral, cut people out of your will, tell them to their faces that you've cut them out, finish that fat nineteenth-century novel that you've been lugging around since the twentieth century, and generally tidy up.

The government statistics on how people die are lavish and fascinating. Let's forget for a moment that it's a catalogue you can't really shop from. And yet you also can't put it down and say "No, thanks" to the whole thing. So what's your pleasure? Or should I say, "Choose your poison"? In 2015 more than 40,000 Americans committed suicide, out of 2.5 million who died of all causes. Of all suicides, 17 percent are, indeed, by poison. (Over half are by firearms.) Women are three times as likely as men to attempt suicide, but men are four times as likely to succeed.

Of injury deaths (which include poisoning), 85 percent are accidental; 13 percent are suicide; 2 percent are homicide. Accidents have been on a roll and now rank number four among all causes of death. Within the general category of accidents, accidental overdoses, mainly of prescription drugs, recently surpassed auto accidents in killing people. Stroke, which used to be third, is now fifth.

The big two are heart disease and cancer, each of which accounts for about a quarter of the Grim Reaper's annual take. "Chronic lower respiratory diseases" (for example, emphysema) trail at a distant third place, with only 6 percent.

Pneumonia used to be called "the old man's friend" because it ended so many lives whose owners were finished with them. That role (though possibly not the label) has now been taken over by accidental falls. The death rate from falls nearly doubled from 30 per 100,000 in the year 2000 to nearly 60 per 100,000 in 2013.

And here's a creepy one: The death rate due to suffocation is eight times higher for people over eighty-five than for people between the ages of sixty-five and seventy-four.

Together, cancer and heart disease account for

almost half of all deaths in the United States, so choosing between these two is a good way to avoid disappointment. But an informed choice isn't easy. Heart disease runs the spectrum from a sudden fatal heart attack while opening Christmas presents with your grandchildren to years of bedridden decline. A stroke (number five) could be your best option (you're gone in a few seconds) or among your worst (you're alive for years but unable to move or talk). Nevertheless, among the top five, cancer is clearly the one to avoid. Although often these days people are cured of cancer, the topic here is what kills you, and our premise is that something is going to kill you eventually (a premise with considerable data to back it up). Cancer, if it kills you, is not likely to do so gracefully.

Number fourteen on the government's "best killer list" (as it is not called) is Parkinson's disease. Of the 2.5 million who died of all causes in 2011, 23,000 died of Parkinson's. This interested me, because I have Parkinson's, and one of the first things you are told, at least if you are still middle-aged when you get the diagnosis (I was forty-two; now I'm sixty-five), is that you are not likely to die of it. It turns out that people do die of it, but rarely before very old age, even if they got the diagnosis when fairly young. In 2012, Parkinson's killed another 23,000 Americans. But only 496 were in my fifty-five to sixty-four age group. By contrast, more than 9,000 were over the age of eighty-five. (This is encouraging: Not only do most people with Parkinson's not die of it, but even of those who do, almost half make it past eighty-five.)

Parkinson's is what happens when your brain stops producing enough dopamine. It entails a strange collection of symptoms that are distributed somewhat randomly among its victims. Almost no one has all of them. Everyone has some. It is classified as a "movement disorder," and it certainly is that, though the disorder can take the form of stiffness approaching paralysis or shaking and exaggerated movements approaching an epileptic fit. And there are other symptoms, unrelated to movement, such as insomnia, depression, and bad skin. Some people with Parkinson's have trouble walking through open doorways. (You have to back up and give yourself a running start.) The drugs you take to alleviate the symptoms have symptoms of their own, ranging from involuntary movements of various sorts to (my favorite) a compulsion to gamble.

Even two decades after I got the diagnosis, my symptoms are on the mild side, though no longer unde-tectable. They got even milder after I had an operation to implant wires in my brain and two pacemaker-like batteries in my chest. The batteries send pulses to a particular point in the brain that . . . well, I don't really know much about how it works. But the result is that I take fewer pills than before and have much less "off" time, when the pills don't work. The procedure, known as deep brain stimulation, or DBS, though no longer officially "experimental," was still fairly exotic when I had it about a decade ago. As a treatment for Parkinson's it has become almost commonplace since then. It has been tried on other ailments as well, in-cluding depression, obsessive-compulsive disorder, and even Tourette syndrome. ("No shit," did I hear you say?) For each disease, doctors go for a different spot in the brain. It's almost like phrenology reinvented, with the important difference that DBS works. My surgeon, Dr. Ali Rezai, then of the Cleveland Clinic, is a renowned pioneer in deep brain stimulation and a great enthusiast. I have joked with him that if I came to Ohio complaining of athlete's foot, he'd know just the spot in my head where the wires should go.

During the operation, your head is screwed into a metal frame and the frame is screwed into the operating table. Some surgeons do it without the frame—certainly the most unpleasant part of the surgery—but this sounds to me like machismo (a professional deformity, as the French say, among neurosurgeons). Take my advice and let them screw your head to the table. My surgery lasted nine hours, and for most of it I had to be awake, so that the doctors could test the connection, like asking somebody to go upstairs and see if the light in the bedroom comes back on while you fiddle with the circuit-breaker box in the basement. It's not fun, but it doesn't hurt (your brain has no nerve endings for pain), and everything except the operation itself is sort of fun after all.

Immediately after surgery, all the symptoms of Parkinson's disappear—even though the batteries aren't turned on for a month. The very process of implanting the wires mimics the effect of the electricity from the batteries. Over the next two or three weeks, the old symptoms return. Then, when the batteries are turned on, the symptoms disappear or are reduced again. These results are instantaneous, though they vary from patient to patient, and it takes up to a year of visits, every month or so, to get the adjustment right.

Along with the benefits, there are some minor nuisances. At the airport, I am not supposed to go through the metal detector. Instead, I stand spread-eagled while the TSA man feels me all over, using (he assures me) the back of his hand for "sensitive areas." I am supposed to keep my distance from refrigerator doors—especially those big, heavy Sub-Zero refrigerator doors that virtually symbolize yuppie desire—because they use strong magnets to stay shut, and these can interfere with the batteries. I can usually get a rise out of my wife by walking innocently past our refrigerator and pretending to be sucked toward and pinned against the doors. When I wanted some wireless earphones to use on the exercise machine, every brand I tried crackled with interference. I finally figured out why: my built-in antennae. This is all a small price to pay.

Everything about DBS is improving all the time. They now only need to install the battery on one side, not two. You do have to get the batteries replaced in a minor surgery every four or five years, but the new batteries apparently don't interact with magnets, so you should be able to walk through airport security like a normal person—though they still advise against it.

The future for people with Parkinson's is unclear but in a good way, because that future is getting better. New drugs are coming along all the time. The demographic power of the boomer generation, as it enters the Parkinson's years, will spur more research and new therapies. And of course, there is the promise of DNA and stem cells.

The lost years are maddening, especially since the opposition to stem cell research, if it isn't purely cynical, is based on a fundamental misunderstanding. The embryos used in stem cell research come from fertility clinics, where it is standard procedure to create more embryos than are needed and to dispose of the extras. (For that matter, this is not so different from standard procedure in the method of human reproduction devised by God as well, which relies on spontaneous abortions to weed out the weaker embryos.) Thousands of embryos live and die this way every year, and there is no fuss. Why don't prominent politicians speak out against fertility clinics? If embryos are morally equal to children and adults, fertility clinics are slaughterhouses. President George W. Bush did discuss fertility clinics in his TV speech on stem cell research. He mentioned them in order to praise them for their contribution to human happiness. (In his speech, President Bush announced a ban on federally funded embryonic stem cell research. Obama restored the funding of stem cell research and ended the ban soon after taking office.) You cannot logically be against stem cell research on the ground that it encourages what happens in fertility clinics and yet be in favor of, or indifferent to, fertility clinics themselves. And yet for eight years, that was my country's official position.

Even now that the ban is lifted, stem cell research is unlikely to develop fast enough to bail me out. Nevertheless, I'm optimistic. Unlike other neurological ailments such as epilepsy or multiple sclerosis, which entail flare-ups, Parkinson's tends to advance at a steady pace (relentless, you might say). Factoring in other new treatments, and my good luck so far, I figure that my chance of being alive at eighty—fifteen years from now—is about as good as that of any other sixty-five-year-old American male. That chance is almost exactly fifty-fifty. And I'm more likely to be felled by a heart attack, just like my boomer buddies, than by Parkinson's. On the other hand, the chance that I'll be cross-country skiing in my eighties is small. Not that I ever did much cross-country skiing. One incidental benefit of Parkinson's has been regular opportunities to ring changes on that old joke "Doctor, Doctor, will I be able to play the piano?" (Doctor: "Yes, certainly." Patient: "Funny, I never could before.") When it comes to having the tiniest telephone or the biggest refrigerator, I'm still in the game. But when it comes to the ultimate boomer game, competitive longevity, I'm on the sidelines doing color commentary. This is not because I'm more likely to keel over early but because having a chronic disease—or, more to the point, being known to have a chronic disease—automatically starts you on your expulsion from the club of the living.

Sometimes I feel like a scout from my generation, sent out ahead to experience in my fifties what even the healthiest boomers are going to experience in their sixties, seventies, or eighties. There are far worse medical conditions than Parkinson's, and there are far worse cases of Parkinson's than mine. But what I have, at the level I have it, is an interesting foretaste of our shared future—a beginner's guide to old age.

Many of the symptoms of Parkinson's disease resemble those of aging: a trembling hand, a shuffling gait, swallowing—or forgetting to swallow, or having trouble swallowing—a bewildering variety of pills. Of the half dozen or so main Parkinson's drugs, the most effective by far goes by the trade name Sinemet. Its principal ingredient is levodopa, a chemical that turns into dopamine in the brain. Levodopa works differently for different people, and often stops working or develops intolerable side effects. But for me right now Sinemet's effects last about four hours. During those four hours I go through the whole cycle of life, or at least the adult part. I take a pill and shortly feel as if I am twenty. My mood is sunny and optimistic, I move fluidly, I'm full of energy—I don't know whether to go out and run a couple of miles or finish that overdue book review. This feeling lasts for a couple of hours, then starts to wear off. Another half hour, maybe, and I'm back where I belong, in middle age. Half an hour after that, I'm feeling old, stiff, tired, and gloomy. Then I pop another pill and the cycle starts all over.

I was around fifty when I went public about having Parkinson's, and the effect was more like turning sixty. A person who is sixty and healthy almost surely will live many more years. But sixty is about the age when people stop being surprised if you look old or feel sick or drop dead. (It's another decade or so before they stop pretending to be surprised.) It's often said of people, "She's a young seventy" or "He's thirty, going on forty-five." And it's true: There is your actual, chronological age, and then there's the age you see in the mirror, the age that reflects how you look, how you feel, how much hair you have left, how fast you can walk, or think, and so on. At every stage of life, some people seem older or younger than others of the same age. But only in life's last chapter do the differences get enormous. We are not shocked to see a seventy-one-year-old hobbling on a cane, or bedridden in a nursing home, and we are not shocked to see a seventy-one-year-old running for president. The huge variety of possible outcomes—all of them falling within the range considered "normal"—makes the last boomer competition especially dramatic. So does the speed at which aging can happen. Sometimes it's even instantaneous. Fall, break your hip, and add ten years. Do not pass Go, do not collect two hundred dollars. It's easy to imagine two sixty-year-olds, friends all their lives. One looks older because he's bald—no big deal.

Ten years later, when they're seventy, the bald one has retired on disability and moved into a nursing home. The other is still CEO, has left his wife for a younger woman, and, in a concession to age, takes a month off each year to ski. Contrasts like these will be common.

Almost 3 percent of Americans older than sixty-five are residents of nursing homes, and for those older than eighty-five the figure is just over 10 percent. The odds look reassuring—even among the very-oldsters, it's only one out of ten. Trouble is, just being out of a nursing home doesn't necessarily put you in a Mrs. McNamara Memorial Love Shack. Actual nursing homes are just the penultimate stop along a trail of institutions that we boomers have become familiar with—and try not to think about—in dealing with our parents. It starts with so-called independent living, and runs through assisted living to the nursing home, with possible detours through home health care and rehab, and thence to the hospital and points beyond. One admirable goal of these institutions is to ease the inevitable transition from active, contributing citizen to dependent, living off the financial and emotional acorns stored over a lifetime. But these institutions also announce that transition and push people along. Entering one of these places is entering a new phase of life as clearly as going away to college.

Decades before the nursing home, though, we all cross an invisible line. Most people realize this only in retrospect. If you have a chronic disease—even one that is slow-moving and nonfatal—you cross the line the moment you get the diagnosis. Suddenly, the future seems finite. There are still doors you can go through and opportunities you can seize. But every choice of this sort closes off other choices, or seems to, in a way that it didn't use to. In every major decision—buying a house or a car, switching your subscription from *Time* to *The Economist*—you feel that this is the last roll of the dice. It needn't be this way; in the more than twenty years since my own Parkinson's was diagnosed, I've moved half a dozen times, changed jobs even more often, gotten married, let my *New Yorker* subscription lapse and then renewed it. Each change feels like an unexpected gift, or a coupon I'd better redeem before it expires.

This terror of being written off prematurely (like being buried alive) makes it difficult to write about a medical condition that may linger and get worse slowly for decades while you try to go about your life like a normal person. People say, in all kindness, "Hey, you look terrific," which leaves you wondering what they were expecting, or how you looked the last time you saw them. They seem taken aback that you are around at all. The first time you hear or read a casual reference to "healthy persons," it is a shock to realize that you are permanently disqualified for that label. And then you realize—even more shocking—that you're the only one who's shocked. Everyone else has adjusted, reassigned you, and moved on. Even if you feel fine, you walk around in an aura of illness.

By a weird coincidence, my aunt, who knows nothing about this book, sent me an artifact she'd come across in the process of moving my uncle and herself from the small house in Uniontown, Pennsylvania, where they had lived for decades and raised four children, into a gargantuan independent-living facility outside of Washington, DC, near some of her grandchildren. It is a letter I apparently sent to a cousin at age sixteen, filling her in on important developments. After describing possible summer jobs et cetera, the letter concludes, "I forgot to mention what's really exciting. I can drive now! And I took the test on four hours' sleep. Nothing else new."

Driving makes you a grown-up. Precisely because you are trying to lead a normal life, and believe you are succeeding, the first really big shock, the first real change in your life and unambiguous message that you're ill, comes when you are told that you have to give up driving. This changes your life dramatically—and not in a good way. The driving issue is one of the big ones between spouses, and between parents and adult children. Even if it comes when you're in your late eighties, and even if you know it's probably necessary, you resent it terribly. When it happens in your early sixties, it immediately drops a fence between you and all of your age-cohort friends. They can drive; you can't. None of this is completely rational. Rationally, you should realize that the process of aging, with or without a major ailment, will gradually rob you of many things more important than your driver's license. Still, it's depressing to think of all the places you never went to because it seemed like too much trouble to drive there. Meanwhile, because your family and friends have most likely processed the fact of your health problems more thoroughly than you have, and have come to terms with them, which you haven't, they can't understand why you are so upset and resist so mightily. You've got Parkinson's—did you think you'd never have to stop driving? Or, as the late Meg Greenfield put it, "Other people's troubles are always easier to bear."

In these family discussions, Granny is on the defensive. She is the one with the biggest incentive to ignore reality. Although I have stopped driving, at my wife's insistence, I still believe that I'm a better driver than she is. But the thought of arguing about it, and the thought that one accident could prove me disastrously wrong, persuaded me to give in without much of a fight.

I've found what many people find who give up or curtail their driving, even those who do it with no medical compulsion: The combination of walking and public transport can get you where you need to go more cheaply than buying, maintaining, and fueling a car. It takes a bit longer—but often only a bit. It helps if you can afford to treat yourself to a taxi or Uber when necessary, or even when not necessary, just because you feel like it.

Rationally, giving up driving is one of the lesser

deprivations that are imposed on people for one reason or another. In fact, it is one of the lesser sacrifices that you yourself will have to make as you get older. But it doesn't feel that way when it hits you. As I say, this is partly because it is often the first big one. Also partly because a car represents freedom. But partly because a driver's license represents adulthood, and full participation in adult life. Not being able to drive infantilizes.

Studies confirm the obvious: It's depressing to stop driving. There is a correlation between Parkinson's and depression anyway. Over half of all Parkinson's patients are clinically depressed—and not just because it's depressing in the nonscientific sense; there's something chemical going on—they don't know what. Add to this the conclusion of one study involving four thousand elderly men and women—that turning in your keys makes you 44 percent more likely to "experience increased depressive symptoms"—and you've got a fine formula for a pretty dismal Saturday night. Other studies of the perfectly obvious have concluded that people who give up driving have lower levels of life satisfaction than either those who are still driving or those few who never drove. That's after correcting for age, medical condition, median time for a pizza to be delivered, and everything else. Big surprise.

People with Parkinson's often develop a blank, un-blinking stare known as "facial masking." They also tend to mumble. Symptoms like these can lead friends and family to think that those with Parkinson's are losing their wits. Cognitive problems affect an uncertain percentage of Parkinson's victims, primarily those who get the disease late in life. But, as discussed in the next chapter, researchers have concluded that cognitive problems are more central to Parkinson's than was previously believed.

Some researchers believe that "young onset" Parkinson's, meaning diagnosed before the age of fifty, may be an entirely different disease. But of course you can't count on everybody you meet in a day being totally up to speed on the latest research about a disease they don't have. The familiar dream that you are in the middle of an exam you haven't prepared for has some basis in reality for a person with Parkinson's, just as it must for many people in their seventies and for almost all those in their eighties. In every social encounter, you're being observed and assessed. Twenty years ago I was described in a *New Yorker* profile as having "a languid, professorial air . . . his arms stiffly by his side; his eyes seem stretched open, for he seldom blinks, and . . . [he] speaks slowly, deliberately, quietly [with] parsimonious gestures." Since I've gone public, no one has suggested that these symptoms add up to looking "professorial."

For a yuppie careerist, the first painful recognition that you have crossed an invisible line from being healthy to being sick probably comes at work. You've done fine, and your boss and coworkers have been as sympathetic as you let them be, but guess what? You've had your last promotion. You will not be chair of the company, or editor of the newspaper, or president of the university. To be sure, it's mathematically inevitable that for every CEO there will be half a dozen vice presidents whose careers will seem successful enough to everybody but themselves. Nevertheless, to them the realization that they won't make it all the way to the tippy-top is poignant. For someone with a chronic disease, it's slightly different. It's not that the arc of your career never quite reached the apogee that you hoped for. It's that the arc was unexpectedly chopped off. (Why that should seem more unfair, I cannot say. But it does.) For most people the realization comes when somebody younger gets a job that they covet. For the person with a chronic disease, it's when somebody older than you gets the job. You're over. He's still a player. He wins.

Timing is everything. Shortly after becoming chief justice, John Roberts had the second of what appeared to be epileptic seizures. The first had occurred fourteen years earlier. No one even suggested that he should have to resign from the court. But do you think President Bush would have nominated Roberts if the second seizure had already occurred? Unlikely. Why risk it?

It is a treasured corollary of the American Dream that most people who are successful in midlife were losers in high school. As you enter adult life, values change and the deck is reshuffled. You get another chance and maybe, if you're lucky, the last laugh. But it isn't the last laugh. The deck is shuffled again as you enter the last chapter. How long you live, how fast you age, whether you win or lose the cancer sweepstakes or the Parkinson's bingo—all these have little to do with the factors that determined your success or failure in the previous round. And there is justice in that.

Some people win two rounds, or even all three. But they, too, cross that invisible line at some point. Old soldiers aren't the only ones who just fade away. What ever happened to Robert McNamara anyway?

5

HAVE YOU LOST YOUR MIND?

"Write about what you know," the creative-writing teachers advise, desperate to avoid having to read twenty-five stories about robots in love on Mars. And what could you know better than the inside of your own head? Answer: almost anything. And almost anyone else is better positioned than you are to write about the foreign land between your ears. You are the person least qualified to be writing about changes in your own brain, since you need your brain to comprehend those changes. It's like trying to fix a hammer, using the hammer you're trying to fix. Without getting into robots on Mars, I remember vaguely, from the 1960s, a comic-book tale about some residents of our three-dimensional world who go through a hole in space, or something like that, and find themselves living in two dimensions. "And nothing's changed," one says triumphantly, unable to see what we can see: that he is now the approximate shape and depth of a postage stamp. Maybe this is what the descent into dementia is like: Everyone around you knows or suspects you have it, but to yourself you seem unchanged.

The tsunami of dementia that is about to swamp us as the baby boomers age has gotten plenty of attention, but the reality has not sunk in. We stave it off with jokes: Ronald Reagan goes in for his annual physical and the doctor says, "Mr. President, I have bad news and worse news." Reagan says, "Lay it on me, Doc." The doctor says, "The bad news is that you have cancer." Reagan: "And the worse news?" Doctor: "You have Alzheimer's." Reagan: "Well, at least I don't have cancer." Go ahead and laugh, if you think that's funny. I do, and so did John Sununu, the Republican former governor of New Hampshire and White House chief of staff, when he told it to me. So sure, go ahead and laugh. You're just whistling past the nursing home. We make jokes about Alzheimer's that we never would make about cancer—not because it's the inherently funnier disease but precisely because it isn't. Even a joke about Alzheimer's and cancer is inevitably a joke about Alzheimer's. Cancer is dreadful, and I don't want to challenge anyone to a round of you-think-you've-got-problems. And to be clear from the start, at the cost of giving up the opportunity for some artificial tension and flashy foreshadowing: I don't have Alzheimer's, or any other form of dementia, at the moment. (Well, to update a famous joke from Will Rogers, I have no form of dementia unless you count voting Democratic.) But I do think about it. There is a special horror about the prospect of shuffling down the perennially unfamiliar corridors of some institution in a demented fog, being treated like a child by your children, watching TV all day but unable to follow even the most simpleminded propaganda on Fox News or the most facile plot twist of *Downton Abbey*. Dementia seems like an especially humiliating last stop on the road of life. There's no way to do it in style or with dignity. And you can't be sure that you're going to avoid it until the moment something else, like cancer or a big, big truck, comes along to carry you off first. Baby boomers—the 79 million Americans born between 1946 and 1964—will be the second dementia generation, but they are the first to know what's coming. Our grandparents generally died too young or too poor to worry about what used to be called "senility." They didn't provide much in the way of foreboding for their children, who are our parents. For us, however—the boomers, now in our fifties, sixties, and seventies—the challenges, financial and psychological, of dealing with infirm and often mentally impaired parents are the fly in the ointment of what is otherwise a pretty good lifestyle. By now there is an extensive literature, fiction and non-, about watching your parents lose their minds. There are books by and about people losing their own minds, too. But they tend to be rock stars or drug addicts or both, already famous for their dissipation. These are people who have some prior claim on your prurient interest, not real people whose experience can strike fear in your heart (or, rather, your brain) that "This could happen to me."

But it can. And it will, to millions of people who have never taken drugs or misbehaved in any serious way. They are jogging every day but will get Alzheimer's anyway. So you need to recalibrate. Is it simply long life that you covet, or is it long life with all your marbles? Isn't the final boomer game really competitive cognition?

The rules of competitive cognition are simple. The

winners are whoever dies with more of their marbles. "He was a hundred and two years old when he was accidentally shot by a neighbor, and except for his habit of breaking into nearby homes and stealing the booze, he was still sharp as a tack." That's the kind of thing you want said about you. So "Death before dementia" is your rallying cry. It is also your best strategy, at the moment, since there's no cure for either one.

Of the 79 million boomers, 28 million are expected to develop Alzheimer's or some other form of dementia. (Alzheimer's is the most common, followed by stroke, the festively named dementia with Lewy bodies, and injury. Parkinson's comes fifth.) That adds up to about 35 percent, or one out of three, and the only reason the number isn't higher is that many people suffering from dementia die of something else first. Similarly, longer life is probably the only reason that women are more likely than men to suffer from dementia. (A sixty-five-year-old woman has a 17 percent chance, versus 9 percent for a sixty-five-year-old man.) Anyone who lives past eighty-five, as more and more of us intend to, has roughly a fifty-fifty chance of exiting by way of Alzheimer's. So there are two forms of competition in the boomer death-style Olympics. There's dying last and there's dying lucid. And in a really nice touch by whoever designed these games, the better you do in one, the worse you're likely to do in the other. If you're prepared to die at sixty, you can pretty much scratch dementia off your list of things to worry about. By contrast, if you don't mind being a bit dotty—or worse than a bit—you can go for longevity. But unless you're extremely lucky, you won't win both games.

When I was told that I had Parkinson's disease, I was forty-three. (Michael J. Fox, since you ask, was only thirty when he got the bad news.) After several weeks of quietly freaking out, it occurred to me to wonder whether it would affect my brain. I already knew that this was not the right question. Parkinson's is completely a brain disease, unlike, say, multiple sclerosis, which causes more widespread damage. But I knew what I meant and you know what I mean. Would it affect my ability to think?

I already knew the answer to that one, too, really.

One of the tricks many people with PD learn is that if you're stuck in a chair and can't get up, you imagine yourself getting out of the chair, and then usually you can do it. So I knew that thinking was involved. I asked my neurologist at the time, and he answered carefully, "Well, after a few years you may lose your edge." Lose my edge? *Lose my edge?* Oh, shit! I need my edge. My edge is how I make a living. More than that: My edge is my claim on the world. It's why people are my friends, why they invite me over for dinner, perhaps why they marry me. What am I worth to the world if I've lost my edge? Gradually, I calmed down. My physical symptoms seemed to be advancing quite slowly. Even after twenty-plus years, if I take my meds, I can seem almost symptom-free for most of the day. Sometimes I imagine that I feel my edge dulling, but usually I feel—ominously like those flattened people in the comic book—that nothing has changed. (Recently, a standard-issue baby-boomer bad back has been more burdensome to me than Parkinson's. You'd think that if you've been assigned a major health issue like Parkinson's, you'd get a pass on the minor ones, like a bad back. But it doesn't work that way.)

Meanwhile, my neurologist—a brilliant and warm-hearted man in his thirties, with a family—died of a brain tumor. So you never can tell. You can't even be entirely certain that a diagnosis of Parkinson's is correct until your brain is sliced open at an autopsy, and frankly, I've never been curious enough for that. But

I still retain the tiny, irrational hope that the whole thing will turn out to have been a terrible mistake.

I don't feel as if my mind is working more slowly than it ever did. Or, rather, I don't feel I'm getting slower faster than my boomer friends. Does that mean I'm not? Do you know when you're losing it, like the computer HAL in the movie *2001*?

> I'm afraid, Dave. Dave, my mind is going. I can feel it. I can feel it. My mind is going. There is no question about it. I can feel it. I can feel it.

Or is being demented, even mildly, like having a sign on your back that everyone can read except you?

When I'm blue, I look to role models for inspiration. Did I mention that neurologists generally believe that Hitler had Parkinson's? Francisco Franco and Mao Zedong too, probably. What a trio! These men were demented to be sure, but not necessarily (let's hope) in the way your grandmother is. Nevertheless, it surely must require a superior intellect to become a fascist dictator (unless you inherit the job, like Bashar al-Assad or Kim Jong-un). Other famous Parkinsonians include George Wallace, Enoch Powell, and

Pierre Trudeau. All had big personalities, and maybe that is part of what my doctor meant by "edge." Or how about this one: Thomas Hobbes. He wrote *Leviathan* with the help of secretaries, years after his diagnosis of the "shaking palsy."

Is it just happenstance, I ask you, that both Hitler and Franco were nasty, brutish, and short? Okay, maybe it is just happenstance. And then there's Michael J. Fox, the world's most famous living Parkinsonian (that is, not the most famous person to have had Parkinson's—that would have to be Hitler—but the person most famous for *having* Parkinson's). Michael is neither nasty nor brutish—far from it in either case—but he is undeniably short. There are exceptions, such as Chairman Mao, who was a stately five feet eleven.

All in all, it's an impressive list (although it remains a club I'd just as soon not be a member of). The law of averages does not decree that in any random group of millions of people one or two will turn out to be fascist dictators. In his 2011 book, *The Cognitive Neuropsychiatry of Parkinson's Disease*—pretty much a bad-news read—Patrick McNamara, a neurologist at Boston University (and no relation to the former secretary of defense), writes, "PD, apparently, does not prevent creative work of a very high intellectual caliber."

After some reflection, I concluded that as long as I still felt infallible, Parkinson's would not stop me from continuing to pursue my dream of becoming pope. If John Paul II could do it, why couldn't I? The years passed. I got married, went to work for Microsoft, and concluded that any changes in my cognitive ability were pretty minor, and progressing slowly enough so that the truck with my name on it is almost certain to arrive in time to spare me the grimmer options.

But in the two decades since I got my diagnosis, there has been a revolution in thinking about this still-mysterious disease. Parkinson's has always been classified as a movement disorder. People shake uncontrollably, or they freeze trying to go through a doorway, or they slow down and shuffle when they walk. Mental problems as such were thought to arise only sometimes, after many years. Neurologists now believe that defects (or, as they put it tactfully, "deficits") in cognition, memory, and other popular mental pursuits can predate the physical symptoms that lead to the diagnosis. The medical journals are full of articles with titles such as "The Neglected Side of Parkinson's Disease" and "Parkinson's Disease: The Quintessential Neuropsychiatric Disorder." The non-movement-related symptoms usually are not helped by levodopa, the miracle drug that revolutionized Parkinson's treatment in the 1960s and remains what neurologists like to call the "gold standard." It is the most common drug that works clearly for most people with Parkinson's symptoms, at least for a few years. But now there is some evidence that levodopa can make the non-motor symptoms worse.

McNamara summarizes the current view in a way that other neurologists I've asked, without endorsing it 100 percent, say is fair: "Neuropsychiatric disturbances of Parkinson's disease . . . can be as disabling as the motor symptoms of the disease. Upwards of 85% of PD patients evidence deficits in executive cognitive functions even early in the disease." He says: "Almost half of all patients progress toward a dementing illness that may occur late in the disease. More than half of all patients suffer severe anxiety or depression. Roughly 50% of patients suffer varying degrees and types of apathy, hallucinations, sleep disturbance, and impulse control disorders." I'll stop there, if you don't mind. It doesn't get any cheerier.

Many neurologists believe that there is something identifiable as a "parkinsonian personality." A 1999 article in the *European Journal of Neurology,* about Hitler's Parkinson's, declares flatly, "It has been proved that Adolf Hitler suffered from idiopathic Parkinson's disease." *Idiopathic* means doctors have no idea why someone got it, but it wasn't from getting hit too often on the head. Hitler had "the typical premorbid personality of parkinsonian patients with uncorrectable mental rigidity, extreme inflexibility and insupportable pedantry." This works both ways: More people with Parkinson's display these unattractive traits, and more people with these traits have Parkinson's, or will get it. McNamara piles on: People with Parkinson's have been described as "socially withdrawn, rigid, punctilious, serious, stoic, introverted and uninterested in others."

But enough about him. Let's talk about me. To me, this doesn't sound like me at all. Still, how can I know? Maybe he's got me nailed, but the nature of these traits makes me incapable of recognizing that I've got them. No pedant thinks he's a pedant.

Anyway, there is a more obvious explanation of why someone with the physical symptoms of Parkinson's and the knowledge that those symptoms are inexorably getting worse might feel depressed and anxious. But this, apparently, is not a field where Occam's razor cuts much ice. McNamara declares, "PD patients are impaired. . . . They have difficulty making decisions, developing plans . . . and monitoring and adjusting plans and actions." Is it healthy skepticism or an unhealthy mental defect that makes it hard for me to take some of this seriously? He reports a study showing an "apparent willingness" among a subgroup of Parkinson's patients "to associate with a socially untrustworthy individual," along with its near opposite, a tendency of Parkinsonians generally to avoid risks and social interaction, and he attributes both to failures in "mentalizing abilities" (otherwise known, I believe, as thinking). McNamara concludes his discussion of the various "deficits" in the parkinsonian mind with a little pat on the brain.

"My own feeling is that PD patients tend to be

exceptionally intelligent individuals." Unfortunately, he says, "there are no controlled studies that can yet support this claim."

How could experts have failed to notice until the past two decades that Parkinson's is as much about cognitive problems as it is about physical ones? In fact, I would say that there are three categories of Parkinson's symptoms: physical symptoms, such as shaking or freezing; cognitive symptoms, such as the number of states you can name in thirty seconds (*go!*), and psychiatric symptoms, such as depression. But even the latest edition of *Neuropsychological Assessment,* the leading text on this topic, says, "Parkinsonism's outstanding feature is a movement disorder with a number of component symptoms." How could neurologists have missed all this?

The explanation is partly that the motor effects usually become evident before the mental ones and partly that Parkinson's is usually a disease of old people, who tend to die—of Parkinson's or, more often, of something else—before the mental effects have time to flower. Or they are given a misdiagnosis of Alzheimer's or another kind of dementia.

Not that I'm complaining. Widespread ignorance

about the disease has served me well. One of the worst aspects of Parkinson's (and I suspect this is true of other chronic diseases, especially those affecting the brain) is that everybody around you knows you have it. Although they are well-meaning, their sympathy can be excruciating. (I'm sure mine is, too, when the situation is reversed.) On top of everything else, some physical symptoms of Parkinson's—rigidity, tremors, a blank expression (facial masking, it's called), a stooped posture, slow movements, and others—make you look demented even when you're not. Slurred speech, another symptom, doesn't help. All of this is why I chose, like many, to keep my medical problems under my hat until the symptoms became undeniable. In my case, that was about eight years. And as the cognitive effects of Parkinson's become better known, I intend to change the subject ruthlessly. "How about those Redskins!" It'll be tricky. I'm not entirely sure which sport the Redskins play. But I think I have enough marbles to fake it successfully.

In the early 2000s, when I was running the opinion pages of the *Los Angeles Times,* I found myself in a public dispute with a local activist who believed (correctly) that there were too few women on the paper's op-ed page. Luckily, we did a head count and established that—bad as we were—we had a better record than the *Washington Post* or the *New York Times*. In the course of a heated exchange of e-mails, this person suggested unhelpfully that Parkinson's must be affecting my brain. At that point the battle was over and I had won. It was a horrible thing for her to say, even if there could have been some truth in it. That's "some," not a lot. Among those rushing to my defense was a George Washington University law professor, who said that everybody knows Parkinson's is a movement disorder and has nothing to do with one's mental capacity. Even then I could have corrected him, but I didn't. For twenty years, whenever I heard anyone talking about Parkinson's and cognition, I'd be shrieking inwardly, "Shut up! Shut up. Shut up! Have you lost your mind?" Now here I am doing it myself. Have I lost my mind? Well, that is what we're here to find out.

Unlike Alzheimer's, Parkinson's does not inevitably lead to mental problems. Neurologists believe that people who get Parkinson's at an earlier age are less likely to suffer cognitive problems. The fact that I've had it for twenty-odd years can be argued two ways:

The law of averages decrees that my luck probably won't hold much longer, or I have a slow-advancing case and don't need to worry especially about it.

There is also something called mild cognitive impairment, or MCI. Many people with mild impairment from Alzheimer's or Parkinson's lead reasonably normal lives. They may not be able to explain the regulations about preexisting conditions under Obamacare, but they can write perfectly pleasant editorials about the coming of spring and even subtly gloating obituaries about people who've died sooner and of something else. A writer's work, unlike that of most professionals, is judged on its own merits. If you write a good book, or even a good book review, the assignment editor needn't care about the present or future state of your cognitive ability.

Another difference between Alzheimer's and Parkinson's is that Alzheimer's tends to start its destruction in the parts of the brain affecting memory, whereas Parkinson's starts with what they call the executive function: analyzing a situation and your options and making a decision. I've asked several neurologists whether the executive-function problem is wrong decisions or slow decisions or no decisions. The clearest answer I ever got was all three. Some people think that this is where the physical effects of Parkinson's and the mental effects tend to merge: You just generally slow down.

Does it take me longer to write a column than it used to? Maybe. That doesn't bother me much. But if I couldn't reach a conclusion, or tended to reach the wrong one (leaving aside those people who think I've been reaching the wrong conclusion all my professional life), I would find that quite distressing.

I felt that I needed to know. So I decided (decision crisply made and executed, please note) to have myself tested. How should I match my aspirations with my abilities? Depending on the condition of my brain, should I be looking for a good nursing home? Or should I try to find a worthwhile but relaxing job teaching journalism somewhere? Or should I go for the gold and put together a consortium to buy the *New York Times*?

My motive for undergoing this cognitive assessment was part scientific inquiry, part hypochondria, and part the journalist's reaction to any interesting development—"This would make a great piece." A cognitive assessment is basically like a physical exam except that it's testing your mind, not your body. The challenge is that the doctor can't just poke around your brain saying, "Where does it hurt?" Defects in your thinking must be deduced from the brain's performance. So a cognitive assessment, which can last four or five hours or more, is a series of quizzes, puzzles, and games.

In what's called the Counterfactual Inference Test, cited and discussed in McNamara's book, we meet Janet and Susan, who are having a rough day. "Janet is attacked by a mugger only 10 feet from her house. Susan is attacked by a mugger a mile from her house. Who is more upset by the mugging?" Your choices are (a) Janet, (b) Susan, or (c) Same/can't tell. The test is supposed to measure your ability to imagine alternative scenarios as part of making rational decisions. Besides Janet and Susan, the Counterfactual Inference Test introduces us to other victims of modern life, such as Jack, who misses his train by only five minutes, and Ann, who gets sick in a favorite restaurant. What a crew of losers populates these tests! The cognitive assessment I took in November didn't include Janet, Susan, and their friends. But it included many similar tragic figures. To me, the answer is obviously (c). How can you possibly answer the question of which woman was more upset without knowing more about Janet, Susan, and the circumstances of their muggings?

Who is more upset? That depends on all sorts of factors, among which the distance from the mugging victim's home is not even the most important. Please note that the question is not "Who is likely to have been more upset?" or even "Who ought to be more upset?" It's who actually was more upset. Without more information—or without assuming, implausibly, that Janet and Susan are exactly alike, and that the circumstances of their muggings are exactly alike except for the distance from their homes—it is impossible to know who is more upset. Should we assume that both Janet and Susan have average temperaments? That they are the same age, carry similar amounts of money in their purses, have both been mugged before—or have both not been mugged before? Did either mugger carry a knife or a gun? Did Janet or Susan carry a knife or a gun? Is Janet's husband out of town? Is Susan having an affair with him, and does Janet know it? Any number of factors would go into determining someone's reaction to being mugged. If you wanted to plot every mugging in the past year on a graph, with distance from home along one axis and degree of upset along the other (though I can't imagine why you would want to do this. Are you crazy?), you could generate a nice scatter diagram showing a correlation between the distance of a mugging from someone's house and how upset that person gets when she is mugged. That said, what have you accomplished? There is a positive correlation between any number of things about a mugging and how upset a Janet or a Susan gets. Every case is unique. For example, what if Janet is actually Janet Yellen, chair of the Federal Reserve, and she was walking around with M1 for Q2 in a Trader Joe's bag when she got mugged? Isn't she entitled to government protection? Where the hell were they? She might get very upset even if she was many miles from her house. And rightly so! Is all this just quibbling? I don't think so. I can see perfectly well that the authors of this test are pushing me to choose (a) Janet. A mugging close to your house is scarier than a mugging farther away. I get it. (Or maybe I don't get it. It's easier to run back to your house if it's closer.)

So is (a) the right answer? Or is (a) what, in mental-testing circles, they call a "distractor" and in the real world they call sucker bait? The purpose of a distractor is to tempt you into a cul-de-sac of logical error. To answer the question correctly—or, more precisely, to give the people who write the questions the answer they want—you need to peer inside the brains of many people. Not just Janet and Susan but also the people who write the questions. You have to ask yourself not "What is the right answer to this question?" but, rather, "What do they think is the right answer?" Or "What do they want me to think is the right answer?" Answer: The answer they want is (a). Or maybe not. Maybe it's (b) after all. You can argue it either way. Although actually, you can't argue it either way. You can't argue it at all. There are all sorts of reasons I might get this question wrong, but a cognitive deficit is not one of them. The whole exercise is like something out of *One Flew Over the Cuckoo's Nest,* or even *1984.* ("Janet is more upset about being mugged, Winston. Janet has always been more upset about being mugged.")

However, there's a problem. Eighty-six percent of a control group voted for Janet as "more upset." By contrast, 73 percent of the group being studied—my group—shared my view that "Same/can't tell" is the right answer. There are just too many variables, too many possibilities. This leaves me with some explaining to do. Irrespective of who's right and who's wrong, it is disconcerting that a large majority of one group voted one way and a large majority of another group voted another way, when the only difference between the groups is that one (mine) has Parkinson's.

I am perfectly willing to believe, on almost any subject, that I'm right and a majority of other people are wrong. That's more or less been the basis of my career in journalism. But how do I explain the glaring disparity in judgment between the control group and the subject group, and the shared judgment within each group, in this case? I have no explanation. The doctors have an explanation: Parkinson's disease.

When I decided to have myself tested, I tracked down Mark Mapstone. Twenty-three years ago, when I first panicked about losing my edge, I volunteered to be a guinea pig in a study being done at MIT about Parkinson's and cognition. Mapstone was working as one of the test administrators. I remember that he said, about Parkinson's, trying to be sympathetic, "It's a terrible disease." This was just as I was on the verge of convincing myself that it wasn't such a terrible disease. Nevertheless, we hit it off.

Two decades later I found Mark at the University

of Rochester, where, as an associate professor, he is still doing "neuropsychological assessment"—that is, administering and interpreting these games and puzzles. He seemed glad to hear from me and excited at the prospect of comparing my results from 1993 with my results today. Unfortunately, the old results seem to have been shredded somewhere along the way. But I also took the test twice eight years ago, before and after deep brain stimulation surgery, and I was able to obtain those results. The neuropsychological effects of deep brain stimulation surgery, it turns out, is one of Mark's special areas of interest. For me, this surgery has been a miracle in terms of reducing the physical symptoms of Parkinson's. Mark's research, though, suggests that the surgery affects "working memory," which is the brain function that temporarily stores and manipulates information needed for various cognitive tasks. It's been well known for years that many Parkinson's patients suffer from "tip-of-the-tongue syndrome." They'll have the word they need, or the point they want to make, on the tip of their tongue, and then they lose it. I say "they," but it happens to me fairly often. Once again, here is a resemblance between Parkinson's and simply getting older. When people talk about having a "senior moment," they mean roughly the same thing.

Where were we? Oh yes, I decided to have myself tested. I took the exam at the University of Pennsylvania, which has one of the best movement-disorder clinics in the world. Also, I happened to know the two top neurologists in the department. One of them is Dr. Howard Hurtig, the man who accosted me at the neurologists' convention and asked me who my doctor was. The other is Dr. Matt Stern, with whom I'd done a couple of dog-and-pony shows for Medtronic, the company that makes the DBS pacemaker. I did these for free and enjoyed being listed in the program as "faculty," although my role would be more accurately described as "exhibit."

Obviously, when you sit down to take the exam, you are expected to try hard and do your best. But it's not supposed to be a contest. There's no opponent, and there's no point in cheating. The purpose is to get as clear a picture as possible of your cognitive strengths and weaknesses. Still, my attitude was "Screw all that. I'm going to ace this exam, even if I have to cheat to do it." And I did cheat—or I tried. In one exercise, you're asked to name as many items as possible in some general category, in a limited period. In my hotel room in Philadelphia the night before the test, I Googled a list of fruits and vegetables, which had been the categories twenty-three years ago. I read the list several times that evening and again at breakfast. Unfortunately, this time the test used animals instead of fruits, so that clump of brain matter was entirely wasted. Another test involved guessing something about the next card in a stack as the tester turned the cards over, one at a time. There was a trick to this one that made the test easy once you figured it out. I had figured it out twenty-three years ago, and I remembered the gimmick from back then. I said nothing when the tester pulled out her cards, but I put my own cards on the table, so to speak, after the test was over.

The testers were so impressed by my retention of this memory that they mentioned it twice in their report. Unfortunately, they also noted that though I knew the trick, I still scored badly. I have to be a little vague about the details of these games, because I promised as much to Mark Mapstone. Some people, apparently smarter and/or less scrupulous than I am, have been known to take better advantage of fore-knowledge about the tests than I managed to do, thus distorting the result.

This is less of a problem than you might think, because the main reason people take the test, it turns out, is that they're hoping to qualify for early retirement on disability. So they want to do badly. What brain snobs we are, or at least I am. Here I was trying desperately to demonstrate that my brain was in working order (even if it wasn't), while most people were quite sensibly happy to be thought mentally disabled (even if they weren't) if that meant early retirement and a pile of money from the government.

Whenever I have subjected myself to these cognitive puzzles, I have been struck by how reductive they seem to be and yet how much weight is given to the result. Neuropsychologists really believe that wrong answers to a few questions involving the alphabet demonstrate personality traits and mental abilities (or disabilities) that run deep.

I wish I could say that the whole thing is a fraud. But I can't explain why Parkinson's patients and similar groups seem to travel in packs. They might have the right answer or they might have the wrong answer, but they have the same answer, and it's different from the answer that most "normal, healthy" people have. That's weird. The neuropsychologists say it's because Parkinson's patients share a mental defect of some kind. I don't care for that explanation. But I have no other explanation. And you can't beat a horse with no horse. *So* I have reluctantly concluded that there must be something to all this stuff after all. That made the results of my long morning of cognitive testing, which I received by mail a couple of weeks later, a bit disturbing. I've tried to explain it away, with mixed success. When I took the test, I was answering questions, moving pieces of cardboard around, drawing various shapes with a pencil, and performing other tasks that might seem more suitable for my five-year-old grandson. It went on for about five hours. The testers offered me a break, and I foolishly turned it down. Approaching the end, I was feeling tired, and bored, and impatient. This is evident in my scores on the various tests, which start out high enough but then go sharply downhill. Reflecting on this afterward, I felt strongly that the last hour or so shouldn't count, or that I should be allowed to take those parts again. It turns out, however, that perseverance is a cognitive trait and one of the things being tested. My increasingly random stabs at the right answer as the ordeal came to a close were held against me. That I didn't feel like persevering is my problem, not the test's or the testers'.

So how did I do overall? Bottom line: not bad, but not great. When I took the tests eight years ago, after my DBS surgery, I was "off the charts," as Mark Mapstone said, in nearly every category. This time I did poorly in exactly the categories where someone who's had Parkinson's for twenty years would be expected to do poorly.

The summary of my performance, written by Dr. Kathy Lawler, director of the department that administers the cognitive exam, starts out pleasantly: "Mr. Kinsley is a highly intelligent, friendly, and engaging 62-year-old man ... IQ in the Very Superior Range ... excellent cognitive reserve ... exceptionally strong vocabulary ... His drawing of a clock was fully intact." Yes, they ask you to draw a clock. I did well on that one. But then, when they get to "executive functioning," the whole thing heads south.

This section of the report begins: "Mr. Kinsley's

performance varied significantly across measures of executive functioning. Executive dysfunction ... included poor organizational skills, weak verbal fluency, inefficient problem solving, a tendency to break task rules, and weak working memory." That business about "a tendency to break task rules" does not mean that the testers caught me Googling for answers. All I did was move a piece of a puzzle to see how that changed things, before moving it back. I had no intention of keeping it in the wrong place. I was always going to move it back. Honest! Anyway, they never said you couldn't move the damn pieces. Or maybe they did say it.

Who can remember?

Most unnerving of all was a throwaway line: "In addition, his insight concerning his cognitive weaknesses seemed quite limited."

Now wait a minute. That is a game I cannot win. If I deny any cognitive problems, it just proves that I have them. How unfair is that? They are implying that I don't really want to know the truth. Is that true? Yes, of course it's true. But do they have to rub it in? Anyway, they're confirming that I've got that sign on my back, or I'm the hammer that's trying to mend itself.

I'm the postage stamp that doesn't realize it's lost a dimension.

Reviewing my actual test scores was a humbling, if not horrifying, experience. My IQ is fine (and none of your business, thank you). But some of the other numbers tell a different story. They start out in the nineties but then sink. I don't know which of the dozens of tests these scores even refer to, but I don't like them anyway. I'm not used to numbers like 37, 25, 14, 5, 2 . . . A 2? You've got to be kidding. These are bad numbers. A 2 means that on some test or other I did worse than 98 percent of the population, adjusted for age and education. I look out my office window at the rush-hour crowds. Are they telling me that if you scooped up a hundred people at random and gave them the test that I got a 2 on, ninety-eight of them would do better than me? Geezus.

Mark Mapstone was surprisingly hard-line when I appealed to him on the accusation that I "broke task rules" by moving a piece of a puzzle—even though I was going to put it back, honestly, and just wanted to see . . . well, you know. Mark said, "You knew what the rule was. You should have made that decision before initiating movement. One thing we're looking for is impulse control. Putting action before thinking is the kind of error you made. You did something and then thought about it. That's less efficient and less elegant than planning a strategy." About my condition in general, Mark said, "People who receive a diagnosis in their forties and are now in their sixties—this is absolutely what we would expect to see. If I didn't see this, I would be surprised. In a patient who gets the diagnosis at sixty-five or seventy, you would expect to see these symptoms within five years."

Mark is a Ph.D., not a medical doctor, but he shares one trait with many M.D.s. Although doctors are devoting their lives to helping people get better, they seem to find a strange satisfaction in seeing a disease take its predicted course. "That's perfectly normal," they say. "It's what we would expect."

So what's my prognosis? Parkinson's is a degenerative disease, so things are not likely to get better. But they're really not so bad now. How bad could a symptom be if it takes a five-hour test to find it? Mark Mapstone says, "In general, I think that if one looks hard enough, it's possible to find deficits in many people, presumptively cognitively normal or otherwise.

Understanding the brain mechanisms of cognitive diversity and how to fix them when they break is what pushes us forward." Mark was blunt about my low scores in important areas. "Anything from 25 to 75 is considered normal, and that covers many of your low scores, but someone like you, who was doing 95 or 98 eight years ago, normally should be doing better." As for the 5s and 2s, those represent real deficits.

Fortunately, there's my excellent "cognitive reserve," a sort of rainy day fund or unused surplus of brainpower that's there for when I need just a bit more for special projects. Used responsibly, my reserve should see me through—especially if I remain an outlier in terms of the disease in general.

The politically correct line on intelligence (or, as we say in the neurology biz, cognition) is that it's not a single thing—IQ—but rather a collection of talents and abilities that we all have in different amounts. People say this, but I'm not sure how many actually believe it. The notion that intelligence is a number, a place somewhere on the spectrum from stupid to smart, is just too deeply rooted. We say, "She's as sharp as a tack" or "You're not too smart, are you? I like that in a man" (Kathleen Turner, in *Body Heat*). Nobody I know says, "She's great at counterfactual inference but not so great at naming fruits."

What we're learning from the study of cognition is that the politically correct line is actually closer to the truth. There are all sorts of things going on in our heads—and I mean our physical heads, not our minds—that affect how we act or even who we are. This extreme mechanical view can be disheartening. That edge that I'm so vain about is just an extra spritz of some chemical in my brain? But the mechanical view is comforting, too. It says that each of us is a collection of mental strengths and weaknesses: normal people as well as people with chronic degenerative neurological diseases. And weaknesses can be overcome, to some extent, by strengths somewhere else.

People understand this about physical disabilities. Someone with a broken leg will not, for that reason alone, be denied a job that requires typing. We are comfortable with the idea that physical health is not just a single number but a multiplicity of factors. That's where we need to arrive about mental problems, too. As we get older, we're all going to lose a few of our marbles. As the word gets out that Parkinson's disease is not just a movement disorder, there will be people whose careers will be destroyed because, on a particular day at a particular time, they can't recite a seven-digit telephone number backward. Allowing someone's fate to depend on performance on some test that has nothing to do with the job in question is just the reductio ad absurdum of the meritocratic machinery that has been pretty good to me (and to you, I suspect) over most of a lifetime.

6

THE VANITY OF HUMAN HOPES (REPUTATION)

Mark Twain wrote, in reviewing a collection of humor writing:

> This book is a very interesting curiosity, in one way. It reveals the surprising fact that within the compass of these forty years wherein I have been playing professional humorist before the public, I have had for company seventy-eight other American humorists. Each and every one of the seventy-eight arose in my time, became conspicuous and popular, and by and by vanished. A number of these names were as familiar in their day as are the names of George Ade and Mr. Dooley to-day—yet they have all so completely passed from sight now that there is probably not a youth of fifteen years of age in the country whose eye would light with recognition at the mention of any one of the 78 names.

Twain went on, somewhat complaisantly, to list a dozen or so sample forgotten names, of which I recognized none. In fact, to be honest, I also didn't recognize George Ade, who was Twain's example of a name anyone would recognize, and I only recognized Dooley because I assume Twain is referring to Mr. Dooley, the man who famously said, "The Supreme Court follows th' election returns"—one of the great clichés of American political commentary, especially notable for being completely wrong. (When people complain about the Supreme Court, the complaint is almost always that it has failed to follow the election returns.) But who exactly was Mr. Dooley? I have only the vaguest idea.

Humor writers—except for a few of the very best—are not the only writers doomed to obscurity. Almost all writers are. Certainly that includes all those (like me) whose lifetime output mainly has been a thousand words or so a week commenting on current affairs. Trouble is, current affairs tend not to stay current. I wrote a scintillating column many years ago devastating (in my view) the *Wall Street Journal*'s analysis of the Boland Amendment. And it ran in the *Wall Street Journal* itself, which was especially satisfying. I remember all that. What I can't remember is what the Boland Amendment was. It seemed important at the time.

As an experiment, if you ever find yourself in a modern media newsroom or studio, snare a couple of the denizens and ask them if they've ever heard of someone named Joseph Kraft. The correct answer is, "Who?" Or at least that is the answer you're likely to get from anyone born after 1964, the year the baby boom officially ended. The oldest of these post-boomers are just turning fifty and will soon be running the show, if they aren't already.

Post-boomers—Generation X, Generation Y, the Millennials—constitute the vast majority of the working population. The youngest reporters starting their careers this fall were born around 1993, the year Bill Clinton took office. On September 11, 2001, they were about eight years old. They have never written a story on a typewriter. And almost none of them have ever heard of Joseph Kraft.

So who was Joseph Kraft? He was one of the best-known newspaper journalists of his era, which was the 1970s and 1980s. His syndicated column appeared in more than two hundred newspapers, he wrote often for *The New Yorker,* he was often a commentator on television talk shows, and he was the last columnist to have a lock on the so-called Walter Lippmann spot—upper left corner—on the *Washington Post* op-ed page, twice a week. You've surely heard of Walter Lippmann, right? But do you know anything about him? Once upon a time he was a newspaper columnist even more famous than Joseph Kraft. Let's leave it at that.

When the boomer journalists who are just now starting to retire or die first came to Washington, Kraft was a big, big deal. The biggest. James Fallows (now surely I don't have to . . . okay). Fallows is one of the most respected journalists in Washington today. He has been writing for *The Atlantic* for decades, producing a shelfful of books on a wide variety of topics. He was Jimmy Carter's chief speechwriter until he quit and wrote a highly critical article about Carter's governing style.

And who was Jimmy Carter? Well, even Millennials know that. I hope.

When I came to Washington in the late 1970s, the names to reckon with were people such as Joe Kraft,

"Scotty" Reston, Mary McGrory, David Broder, Sally Quinn, "Johnny" Apple, Meg Greenfield, the team of Evans and Novak. I'm probably forgetting some equal big shots, but that just demonstrates my point. All except for Sally Quinn are both gone and forgotten. Today probably a lot more people (certainly a lot more journalists) have heard of James Fallows than have heard of Joseph Kraft. Kraft died in 1986 at the age of sixty-one, which is certainly insufficient, and was almost immediately forgotten by all except his close friends and family. This is the same group that remembers each of us—we hope. Joe Kraft, I'm fairly certain, hoped for more. I do too. Neither one of us is likely to get it.

In 1975, even before he worked at the White House, the young Jim Fallows established his reputation by writing an article for the *Washington Monthly,* a profile of Joseph Kraft, called "The Most Famous Journalist in America." It memorably began, " 'I think I'm good,' said Joseph Kraft, and paused to pick up the phone." And it was downhill from there. The title was tongue-in-cheek, based on an anecdote, but it wasn't that far off the truth. It's hard to believe that James Fallows will ever tumble into the obscurity that has enveloped Joseph Kraft, who is better remembered today for having been married to Polly Kraft, a prominent and talented painter who later married Lloyd Cutler, Washington's leading lawyer/lobbyist. It's hard to believe that the same obscurity awaits such Washington journalist superstars as Maureen Dowd and Tom Friedman. But it probably does.

Even the most successful people die eventually, and they spend longer dead than they did alive. So the real, ultimate, final boomer competition is not about living large or living long, or living lucid. It's about reputation.

In her 2015 book, *Those Who Write for Immortality: Romantic Reputations and the Dream of Lasting Fame,* H. J. Jackson, a professor at the University of Toronto, takes up the question of literary reputation. She defines *fame* as something that either happens or doesn't happen during your lifetime, whereas reputation is what happens after you're dead. Although she is admirably fair-minded, it's clear where Jackson comes down: There's little point in writing a book, she believes, unless you're hoping for immortality—hoping, that is, that it will be read after you're gone. (Jackson's previous book was about marginalia—the notes that people write in the margins of books—so perhaps Jackson herself is not going for the gold.)

That said, she reluctantly concedes that Jane Austen is probably a better novelist than Mary Brunton. Who is Mary Brunton? You see, that's exactly the point. You've never heard of Mary Brunton (or at least I never had), but you've read all of Jane Austen again and again. Now, why is that? Could it be that Jane Austen is a much better writer than Brunton? Jackson concedes that talent helps, but only as a matter of "threshold competence." The two novels that Brunton wrote before dying in childbirth were, as Jackson and some of the reviewers of her own book concede, atrocious. Yet according to Jackson, for forty years, covering most of the first half of the nineteenth century, Brunton was regarded as the superior novelist.

Superior to Jane Austen! How can that be? The story of Brunton's decline and Austen's rise, as told by Jackson, demonstrates that even after your own death your family and friends can do wonders for your reputation and even—if you're very lucky—make you immortal. Austen had a family publicity operation working on her behalf. Brunton didn't, and this, Jackson says, made all the difference. Not many readers of Brunton's books will be convinced that it made *all* the difference, but Jackson makes a compelling case that it certainly didn't hurt.

Austen died in 1817, Brunton the next year. But the forces of historical revisionism didn't really start operating until the 1860s. The key event was the publication of *A Memoir of Jane Austen* by James Edward Austen-Leigh, her nephew, in 1870. Jackson describes it as "very much a family affair," with contributions by sisters and nephews. Austen-Leigh himself barely knew Jane Austen. He was twenty when she died and over seventy when *A Memoir* was published. "Family industry carried the project of documentation and memorialization well into the twentieth century," Jackson writes, "when it was taken over by professional scholars."

For fifteen hundred years, Jackson says, it was thought that a book or an author became certified as great through a slow sifting process—a democratic one, in which more and more people of each generation came to believe in them. But that began to change, Jackson says, to Brunton's detriment, when "a widespread belief" grew up that "a work that pleased many in its own day could not, almost by definition, be a work that would last for all time." This is an attitude that is familiar today, perhaps one root of the distinction between highbrow and lowbrow that we are now so comfortable with. Jane Austen is one of the few authors who bridge that gap.

Jackson insists that "what happened to Brunton— the gradual fading and extinction of her name—could easily have happened to Austen. From the vantage point of the 1860s, it might have seemed inevitable that it should. But as we all know, exactly the opposite happened: far from declining, the reputation of Jane Austen began an upward climb that looks, a century and a half later, as though it will never end."

Jackson is a Samuel Johnson scholar, so don't try throwing at her Dr. Johnson's famous line "No man but a blockhead ever wrote, except for money." She says Dr. Johnson may have gotten carried away by a clever phrase and was unable to resist temptation. It can happen to anyone. Jackson allows that Johnson may have been in the mood to be "deliberately contrary." Or it might have been part of his "war on cant."

It's hard to say why it should seem more noble to write for reputation than to write for money, but somehow it does. So Johnson may have found the opportunity irresistible to cut through all that crap. At any rate, he also wrote, "No place affords a more striking conviction of the vanity of human hopes than a publick library." It's clear he's not referring to human hopes for more money. He means the hope of popular success and lasting readership.

Jackson and Johnson agree that the test of immortality is one hundred years. If you make it to a century after your death, you're probably okay for the rest of time. Jane Austen is home free.

So who wins the Lifetime Achievement Awards in the Boomer Hall of Fame? Not the fellow with the most possessions. Not the woman who lives the longest, which could just mean fifteen years staring at the TV in the nursing home, not even noticing for the last ten that the TV isn't on. What's the right formula? What should one want? Is it longevity plus cognition? Live till you're one hundred with all your faculties intact and then get run over by that bus? And remember, we're talking selfishly here. We're not interested in the right formula for Gandhi, or even Robert

McNamara, who spent decades working on expiation for the sins of his middle age. We're talking about you, just another baby boomer—a nice guy or gal, neither angel nor devil. Once you're dead, will the competition finally be over? Not quite. There's still reputation. How will you be remembered after you die? That's all you've got. And you're going to be dead a long time— longer than you've been alive. So it's important. And most challenging of all, the arrangements have to be made—and paid for—while you're still alive. Once you're dead, it's too late.

The challenge of posthumous reputation is really twofold. You want to be remembered favorably, of course, but first you need to make sure that you'll be remembered at all. Most people aren't.

Not everybody is a writer, seeking immortality through words that live on. Non-writers seek immortality by other means. Some individuals reach the unfortunate but not entirely irrational conclusion that the best way to be remembered is by assassinating somebody whose long-lasting fame is guaranteed. There is something very modern about this approach. In the celebrity culture where we all live, nothing is worse to some people than the idea of dying unknown and staying that way. Shooting your way out of this box is a method of leeching off of someone else's celebrity. In the celebrity culture, a negative reputation for all times is better than no reputation at all. John Wilkes Booth shot Abraham Lincoln because he (Booth) was a Southern partisan. John Hinckley shot Ronald Reagan because he wanted fame, like Travis Bickle in the movie *Taxi Driver*—or at least an opportunity to touch fame.

It's hard to think of any way for a normal, middle-class person to establish a good reputation as quickly and efficiently as you can establish a bad one. The best way to gain a healthy posthumous reputation is to get rich and then buy one. In ancient cultures you built a memorial to the gods, which was actually a memorial to yourself. In modern America you achieve the same thing by seizing on what is called a "naming opportunity."

A naming opportunity is the chance to get a building named after you at some charitable institution such as a hospital or theater or university. It will come with some lapidary indication that you paid for it. It's all quite clinical. For X dollars you can get the entire building, though X is usually somewhat less than the entire cost and is usually negotiable. For some smaller fraction of X you can get a wing or a "pavilion" (as hospitals call them for some reason) or a classroom or an operating theater or a seat in an auditorium. Some cultural institutions implant floor tiles with contributors' names on them. Congratulations. You have achieved immortality. Forever people will be walking across your name, and maybe one or two out of thousands of concertgoers will devote a couple of seconds to wondering who the hell you were. At the very least you can get your name on a long list on a plaque on the wall. I say "the very least" but that's not quite correct. At the very least you get no recognition at all beyond a computer-generated thank-you letter from the vice president for development. See how far that gets you on judgment day.

Almost always, while development officers are grateful for the money to help build a new building, what they really need are funds for general expenses and maintenance. But general expenses and maintenance are not glamorous. They're not sexy. They do not suggest fame and immortality, even though immortality and maintenance are close friends in real life.

Although having your name etched in marble may

suggest permanence, the real message of a sign declaring this to be, say, the Travis Bickle Center for Dispute Resolution is nearly the opposite of permanence. It's the lesson of Shelley's "Ozymandias." (You know: "My name is Ozymandias, King of Kings/Look on my Works, ye Mighty, and despair!")

Then, too, if you're buying immortality, you'd better find out how much immortality you're getting. When New York's Lincoln Center for the Performing Arts opened in 1962, its auditorium for orchestra concerts was called, simply, Philharmonic Hall. A few years later, dissatisfied with the acoustics, officials solicited a large gift from Avery Fisher to redo the place and, in return, agreed to change the name to Avery Fisher Hall. Who's Avery Fisher? That's exactly the point. He owned a speaker-manufacturing company, but almost no one knows that. What they know is that the concert hall is called Avery Fisher Hall.

But in 2015, Lincoln Center announced that it was, once again, redoing the hall to improve the acoustics and henceforth it would be named David Geffen Hall, after the media mogul who bought the naming rights. The family of Avery Fisher sold them back for $15 million. So much for immortality.

The Catholic Church used to deal in "indulgences," which were a quite explicit trade-off of money for forgiveness of sins. It's not quite so easy today, but contributions to good causes still serve to cleanse a soiled reputation. And the terms are generally favorable. That is, you can buy forgiveness for your sins—at least forgiveness in this world—for less money than your sins brought in. It's a sort of sin arbitrage: Someone in the SEC slips you insider information worth $200 million. You use the info to short the company's stock, or whatever, then give $100 million to the state university for a new recital hall and pocket the extra $100 million.

But few boomers are billionaires and somewhat fewer are crooks—so few that their experience really can't be used to support generalizations about the entire generation. For that, we need one last chapter.

7

THE LEAST WE CAN DO

The indictment against the baby boomer generation is familiar, way oversimplified, and only partly fair. In brief: The boomers' parents were "the Greatest Generation," a coinage by Tom Brokaw that looks as if it will stick. Toughened by growing up through the Great Depression, the GGs heeded the call and saved the world in 1941–45. Then they returned home to build a prosperous society. They forthrightly addressed the nation's biggest flaw (race relations), and defeated communism on their way out the door. The GGs' children, the boomers, were "bred in at least modest comfort," as the Port Huron Statement of 1962, the founding document of Students for a Democratic Society, startlingly concedes. They ducked the challenge of Vietnam, so much smaller than the military challenge their parents so triumphantly met. They made alienation fashionable and turned self-indulgence (sex, drugs, rock and roll, cappuccino makers, real estate, and so on) into a religion. Their initial suspicion of the Pentagon and two presidents, Johnson and Nixon, spread like kudzu into a general cynicism about all established institutions (Congress, churches, the media, you name it). This reflexive and crippling cynicism is now shared across the political spectrum. The boomers ran up huge public and private debts, whose consequences are just beginning to play out. In the world that boomers will pass along to their children, America is widely held in contempt, prosperity looks to more and more people like a mirage, and things are generally going to hell.

Nobody actually wants the boomers dead (or at least nobody has been impolitic enough to say so), but many wouldn't mind if they took early retirement. From the day John F. Kennedy said, "The torch has been passed to a new generation," to the day George H. W. Bush headed back to Houston, seven members of the World War II generation occupied the White House, for a total of thirty-two years. The boomers had just two presidents, Clinton and Bush the younger, over sixteen years, before the citizenry said, "That's enough. Let's move on." Barack Obama, born in 1961, is technically a boomer (the baby boom unofficially lasted from 1946 to 1964) but consciously ran against a version of boomer values and got a lot of self-hating boomer support as a result.

A couple of years ago a *Wall Street Journal* article quoted from some commencement speeches in which prominent boomers (Indiana governor Mitch Daniels, *New York Times* columnist Tom Friedman, for example) apologized for their generation. Daniels (born 1949) said that boomers as a generation have been "self-absorbed, self-indulgent, and all too often just plain selfish." Friedman (born 1953) said his was "the grasshopper generation, eating through just about everything like hungry locusts." Filmmaker Ken Burns (born 1953) summarized: The baby boomers "squandered the legacy handed to them by the generations from World War II."

Whether fair or not, this will be the baby boom generation in a sound bite unless boomers act to change it.

This same story could be told with a different spin, of course. The so-called Greatest Generation came back from World War II to create a bland, soul-destroying prosperity, unequally shared, and then mired us in Vietnam, a war that should never have been fought. It was the boomers, not the Greats, who forced the nation to address civil rights. And it was the Greats, not the boomers, who got us addicted to debt. The GGs' willfully blind sense of entitlement turned the government—and many private companies, too— into machines for taking money from working people and giving it to "seniors" (in amounts far in excess of what they had contributed). The collapse of the Soviet Union happened on their watch, but this victory was devalued by McCarthyism, the blacklist, CIA misbehavior, and, ultimately, Vietnam and Watergate. The Greats were the ones who got us into Vietnam, and the boomers were the ones who got us out. They did this by convincing a majority of the country that it was a mistake, which it was. (Their disinclination to kill and die for a mistake was, if not noble, certainly not cowardly.) Even as they "sold out" and eased into middle-class life, they changed it for the better. They made environmentalism, feminism, and gay rights so deeply a part of middle-class culture that the terms themselves seem antiquated. They created an American popular culture—particularly music—that swept the world and still dominates. They created the technological revolution that revived capitalism. And they did their share of sacrificing: They paid for their schooling with student loans, becoming the first generation to enter adulthood already burdened by large debts. They also paid, publicly and privately, for their parents' generation to retire in greater comfort than they themselves can reasonably expect. And now— talk about selfishness—many boomers are supporting their children, too, into their twenties and beyond.

Whether the boomers would have risen to the challenge of World War II is impossible to know. But the comparison with Vietnam is misleading. Winning the world war required the total mobilization of society. Vietnam never required more than a small fraction of draft-age men (and of course an even smaller fraction of all draft-age Americans). Most boomers never served their country in the military, because most were not needed. Nevertheless, some of the poison in American politics over the past generation can be traced back to the unfairness of the Vietnam-era draft. *The Atlantic*'s James Fallows presciently predicted this in October 1975, in a *Washington Monthly* article called "What Did You Do in the Class War, Daddy?" Even though almost all of the American soldiers who fought in Vietnam were boomers, and even though there is general (though not universal) agreement that the Vietnam War was a mistake, that boomers from privileged backgrounds mostly avoided the fight has left a vague impression that boomers as a generation failed some test.

But even if the anti-boomer critique is mostly a bum rap, boomers are right to feel at least a bit like a failed generation, because they—at least those who consciously thought of themselves as part of a generation—had hopes. They had an agenda. Peace and love—what ever happened to them? It is a crushing disappointment that boomers entered adulthood with Americans killing and dying halfway around the world, and now, as boomers reach retirement and beyond, our country is doing the same damned thing.

In his 2010 biography of twentieth-century media baron Henry Luce, Professor Alan Brinkley of Columbia discusses Luce's famous 1941 essay, "The American Century," in which he urged Americans to take on the burdens of world leadership, and "to promote, encourage and incite so-called democratic principles throughout the world."

Brinkley, a boomer but usually the most reticent

of narrators, can't resist stepping out of the story at this point to comment that he first read Luce's essay in the 1970s and it struck him as "an obsolete relic of an earlier ... and now repudiated American age. Little did I know how soon its sentiments would be popular again." American exceptionalism—the belief that the rules of nature and humanity don't apply to us—and American hubris about promoting our values in the world got us into Vietnam. This was the analysis of most antiwar boomers. (The ones who rejected America and its values were a tiny minority.) Mainstream boomers believed that Vietnam inoculated us against these vanities and would keep us out of trouble. (Hawks feared they were right.) But the inoculation lasted less than a decade. We started small, with Ronald Reagan's invasion of Grenada, and now, like other imperial powers before us, we're mired in Afghanistan.

But we're still spry. It's not too late for a generational gesture, something that will be the equivalent of—if not actually equal to—our parents' sacrifice in fighting and winning World War II—some act of generosity or sacrifice that will inspire or embarrass the next generation, as the sacrifices and achievements of the Greatest Generation inspire and embarrass many boomers.

So, what'll it be, folks? I'm not the only boomer looking for a redemptive last act. Joe Klein of *Time* magazine, who early on sought the role of chief boomer self-flagellator, wrote a year ago: "For the past several years, I've been harboring a fantasy, a last political crusade for the baby-boom generation. We, who started on the path of righteousness, marching for civil rights and against the war in Vietnam, need to find an appropriately high-minded approach to life's exit ramp."

Klein's answer? You'll never guess: a campaign to legalize marijuana. As the boomers' parting gift to the nation, it's like giving your mom a baseball mitt for her birthday. Klein fantasizes stoned eighty-year-olds toking away their golden years. Legalized marijuana may be a good idea and is coming anyway faster than most people expected. But rocking on the front porch (I mean rocking in a rocking chair) watching the cars go by and uttering an occasional "Oh wow" will not strike many as the equivalent of fighting and winning World War II.

A more popular suggestion, beloved of prestigious commissions and popular among those who worry about our national backbone, is some kind of universal national-service program. This could involve bringing back the military draft (ended in 1973) and combining it with other ways of serving the country, such as teaching, or emptying bedpans at veterans' hospitals. Everyone would be expected to serve when around draft age. This expectation might be enforced by law, but most proponents, in order to maintain the pretense that it's "voluntary," foresee relying on peer pressure and civic hoo-ha, and making participation a condition for getting student loans.

As a monument to the baby boom generation, and in almost every other way, this is a terrible idea, a solution in search of a problem. Most obviously, boomers are now well past draft age. So this is a clear case of "Do as I say, not as I did." Apart from a nice biblical resonance (Abraham offering to sacrifice his son, Isaac), it has little to recommend it. As a way to fill the military, it is almost comically inefficient. Only about 10 percent of American males who were of draft age during the Vietnam War ever went to Vietnam. To make service, military or otherwise, universal would have required coming up with nine do-good or make-work jobs in order to recruit each soldier. Whether a

standby supply of drafted soldiers would make it easier
or harder for a president to get this nation into a war
is, at the least, an open question. Whether the vast majority who do nonmilitary service will likely be doing
work of real value that's now going undone is a question that isn't even open. A universal national-service
program would take jobs away from people who cur-
rently hold them and presumably want them, and
force these jobs on people who don't want them. All to
satisfy some social engineer's vision of what American
society should look like.

So if not legalizing marijuana or reinstituting the
draft, what should the boomer legacy be? It should be
concrete—not "a new spirit of patriotism" or any of
those gaseous high concepts that presidents and news-
magazines resort to when there's not much going on.
It ought to be big. (Remember: The competition is victory in World War II.) It ought to be patriotic. And it
ought to be accomplished by the time the last boomer
turns sixty-five, which would be 2029. Boomers have
thirteen years to redeem themselves.

So what do you give the country that has everything? You give it cash. The biggest peril Americans

now face isn't Islamo-fascism. It's our own inability to live within our means. It would be nice to give our country the wisdom and self-discipline to stop running up the credit card. And we should try. But it's unlikely that we can remake the national character (including our own) in thirteen years. What we can do is offer a lecture and a fresh start. We should pass on to the next generation an America that's free from debt. Instead of ignoring it, or arguing endlessly about whose fault it is and who should pay for it, boomers as a group should just reach out and grab the check.

Besides those who will ridicule this as a silly utopian idea (which it may well be) or oppose it as part of a liberal plot to increase the size of government (which it certainly is not), there will be those who say the whole idea is misguided because we do not need to pay off all these public and private debts. In fact, paying them off would be disastrous, like a large tax increase as the economy is headed into a recession. I'm not going to deal here with these people and this argument, though I believe it's wrong. I'm going to assume that wiping out the nation's debts would be a good thing.

Fair? Of course it's not fair. That's the point. If it was fair, the gesture would be meaningless. Boomers are not primarily responsible for America's debt crisis. Blame goes mostly to the World War II generation, which in this regard was not so Great. They're the ones who notoriously want to "stop the government from messing around with our Medicare," and boomers are the ones who have been paying to support the last vestige of old-fashioned fee-for-service medicine—for the old folks. The boomers themselves and their children are more likely to go to an HMO.

But that's okay. You won World War II, so we are going to take care of your debts, cover your extravagances, and go along with your little pretense that you paid for your Social Security check and you are entitled to it. And to the post-boomer generation, now approaching middle age: We're going to make sure the currency doesn't collapse, or the George Washington Bridge, either, for lack of maintenance. We're going to reduce the national debt down to a reasonable level. We're going to invest in research, catch up with all the deferred maintenance on our physical infrastructure, fix public education. You will not have to be embarrassed by the squalor that greets foreign visitors at our nation's airports.

You're welcome. Just don't let it happen again.

Speaking of squalor, I'm sitting here in a pile of reports and studies by think tanks, public-policy schools, the Office of Management and Budget, and self-appointed grandee fiscal crusaders. They all make the same, tiresomely familiar point: that this can't go on. I don't know how to make that tiresome point vivid and fresh, but Anne Applebaum did pretty well in a rant of a column a few years ago:

> If you don't live in this country all of the time, and I don't, here is what you notice when you come home: Americans—with their lawsuit culture, their safety obsession and, above all, their addiction to government spending programs—demand more from their government than just about anybody else in the world. They don't simply want the government to keep the peace and create a level playing field. They want the government to ensure that every accident and every piece of bad luck is prevented, or that they are fully compensated in

MICHAEL KINSLEY

the event something goes wrong. And if the price of their house drops, they will hold the government responsible for that, too.

She did not add: But they don't want to pay for any of it. Applebaum and I probably disagree about what we want the government to do for us. I'm fine with most of the items on her "no" list. But that debate— about the proper role of government in society—has been rendered almost irrelevant by our refusal to pay for whatever we do choose to order from the menu. Americans have been utterly unrealistic about this. We may legitimately disagree about the timing of any Great Fiscal Cleanup: Do we need a second or third jolt of stimulus first to nail shut the coffin of the Great Recession, adding a trillion or more in IOUs to the pile before turning to the task of reducing the pile? Maybe so. But money well spent is still money spent. The Great Recession may have been a legitimate reason for putting off the day of reckoning—just as a cold may be a good reason to put off a necessary heart operation—but the cold doesn't cure your heart problem or eliminate the need for the operation.

There are a dozen ways to look at the national debt

and the annual government deficit, and they all lead to varying degrees of panic. What's especially scary about our fiscal situation is that everybody knows the facts and concedes the implication, but nobody is doing anything about it except grind out more books.

And the national debt is just a fraction of the problem. State and local governments, unlike the national government in Washington, cannot print money, and many states have constitutions that forbid them to run a deficit. Nevertheless, they will be losing many billions. They'll make up the money by "disinvesting": firing teachers, putting off maintenance on public buildings, shutting libraries. We've been delaying maintenance on our public infrastructure of highways and schools and, yes, airports since at least the 1980s, and the shabbiness is really starting to show. Delaying maintenance is like borrowing against the future. Debt is everywhere you look. Here's a short inside piece in the *New York Times Magazine* about state and local unfunded pension obligations for retired employees. They add up to between $1 trillion and $3 trillion. Until that article, I had given no thought whatsoever to shortfalls in state employee pension funds. You? Now we can only say, "Add it to the pile." Then there is all that consumer debt—those underwater mortgages, those credit cards. And you can pick almost any number you wish, for what Medicare and Social Security will cost above and beyond their alleged "trust funds."

Any use of the word *infrastructure* risks automatically classifying you as a deficit bore. People such as Peter G. Peterson have been lecturing us for years—decades—about the dangers of the national debt, and their terrible predictions have yet to come true. That's correct. But remember Stein's law, named for the late Republican economist Herb Stein: Anything that can't go on, won't. And Americans' piling up of debt—governmental in bad times, like now; personal in good times, like most of the past couple of decades—can't go on.

Who knows how much this whole pile of debt adds up to? Certainly many trillions of dollars. Let's say it equals one year's worth of the nation's output—that is, one year's GDP, or about $17 trillion. That much money would, at any rate, be a big help. Boomers, those lazy, self-indulgent bums, those drugged-out draft dodgers, those mincing flower-power hippies who morphed into Wall Street greedheads with nothing left of their culture of peace and love except a paisley tie: We may not have the opportunity to save the world like our predecessors did, but we can save the American economy from the mess our predecessors are leaving.

If you think of this in the context of normal American politics, any talk of paying off the nation's debts and leaving the next generation with a clean ledger sounds not just boring but insane. (And yet, still boring.) Where are we supposed to get $17 trillion? In this nation of taxophobes, raising taxes by even 1 percent of GDP would be a triumph of leadership, and probably fatal to the career of whoever proposed it. How are we supposed to raise 100 percent of GDP?

However, think of this as an extraordinary historic gesture in response to an extraordinary historic threat to our country and the world. Not a threat like Hitler, perhaps, but a huge threat nonetheless. True, this time it's our own fault. But that recognition does not do anything to solve the problem. So boomers will have to step in. Think of our doing so as one generation's once-in-a-lifetime parting gift to those who follow.

Looked at this way, $17 trillion—it's not so much. A widely noted 2014 study estimated that at least $59 trillion will have been transferred from parents to children and grandchildren between 1998 and 2052. Most of the transfers in the last half of that period will be boomers passing money along to the next generation. But in the first half, money will mostly be coming from the previous generation to the boomers themselves. Boomers could forswear all or part of this unearned inheritance. Or, more realistically, they could allow the government to tax it.

Congress can't resist monkeying around with the federal estate tax, leaving special favors for favored industries and people. In a spectacular display of incompetence, Congress voted as part of George W. Bush's tax cut to eliminate the estate tax for one year only, and then let it revert to what it was beforehand. This year estates of over $5.43 million supposedly pay at a top marginal rate of 40 percent. It's safe to say that anyone smart enough to make $5.43 million is probably smart enough not to have to pay 40 percent. In 2009 the estate tax rose to 45 percent on estates worth more than $3.5 million and raised only $25 billion—in other words, only a small proportion of the population paid it, but the few who did pay really got socked. Or at least the intention was to sock them.

This would not be what I am suggesting here. I

am suggesting a tax that reaches far more people—essentially anyone who inherits any significant amount of money—but at a much lower rate. The principle behind the current estate tax (or once-and-future estate tax) is frankly redistributive: to prevent large private fortunes from growing, generation after generation, with the recipients accumulating power as well as money. It does this very poorly, because of tax shelters and loopholes (all made possible by the power that people with large fortunes have already accumulated). But that's still the idea.

The idea of my tax is to produce a lot of money that can then be used to pay off, or at least buy down, society's debts. If we could collect just 20 percent of the alleged $41 trillion about to pass through two generations, that would be more than $8 trillion.

Critics of the estate tax like to say that it amounts to taxing the same income twice: once when you earn it and again when you die. This is wrong, for the most part. People who leave estates of more than $1 million didn't earn this amount through wages. Most of their fortunes consist of "unrealized capital gains": property (paintings, houses, shares of stock, entire companies) that has become more valuable. As long as they don't sell it, they pay no income tax. And there are plenty of other loopholes to provide untaxed spending money. Most of the people who would be affected by what we might as well call the boomer tax actually did pay taxes when they earned their money originally, because the loopholes and special rates don't apply to plain old wages. These people really will be paying twice, but that's the idea. That's what you do because you didn't have to fight in World War II.

Here is another justification for taxing the money people leave behind when they die. According to a survey from the Federal Reserve Board, the average American household aged sixty-five to seventy-four has assets worth more than $1 million. Typically these amounts get spent down as people get older and sicker, so let's say the second member of the typical couple dies leaving $500,000. That is far below the threshold for the estate tax. But for years this couple has been collecting benefits from Social Security and Medicare. These are supposed to be insurance programs. Social Security protects you against the risk of being old and poor. Medicare protects you against the risk of being old and sick. Medicare operates like typical insurance: It pays to cover the costs of medical care, and it pays out only if you actually are sick and suffer these costs. Social Security is different: It pays whether or not you're actually poor.

But if a couple dies leaving assets worth half a million dollars, the risk they were insuring against—poverty in old age—evidently didn't materialize. The money they received from Social Security, aimed at covering that risk, is instead passed along to their boomer children. That, surely, was never the idea. Why shouldn't they give it back? Or some part of it? Social Security sent out checks worth $863 billion last year, so there is real money here.

This involves all sorts of practical problems, of course. The big one is that you're creating an incentive for old folks to spend down their nest eggs rather than let the money go back to the government. But then, as with proposals for universal national service, the government has two ways to induce desirable behavior. One is to legally require it. The other is the kind of combination of negative and positive inducements that supporters of national service tend to favor. Maybe returning the unused portion of your parents' Social Security could become a social norm. Fashion and peer pressure might be more effective than a law.

One final thought: As we learned during the health-care debate, citizens of other advanced countries live longer than Americans, while spending far less per person on health care. How can that be? Well, it's partly that they don't try to save people through heroic, expensive, long-shot efforts, most of which fail. You've seen the figures: For example, last year Medicare spent $50 billion on the last two months of life. Trouble is, we don't know when we're two months from the end. CBS's *60 Minutes* reported last year that "20 to 30 percent" of this $50 billion "may have had no meaningful impact." Of course, all $50 billion had very little meaningful impact, if the patient died within two months. It's easy enough to be in favor of not paying for treatments that do nothing. The tough decisions involve treatments that do something, but not much. Or treatments they're not sure about.

Even putting costs aside, if you could choose at the beginning of your life which health-care system you'd prefer to live under, you'd pick the one where you'd probably live longer, no? Yes, that medical system involves "rationing," but rationing already goes on here, more than we admit. Why not make it official? Let's be honest: Such a system would cost some boomers their lives, but they would die in their eighties or nineties, unlike the teens and twenty-somethings who gave their lives in World War II. Just a thought.

Boomers: We're all in this one together. You may be wondering, What's stopping Mike from tearing up his Social Security checks (when they start to arrive— still a year off!) or walking around with a permanent Do Not Resuscitate order tattooed on his chest? The answer is, I'm not doing this alone. That would not achieve the purpose of vindicating a generation. Anyway, democratic government is a way of saying "I will if you will."

In case you haven't figured it out yet, I'm not really pushing for boomers to raise $17 trillion and use it to pay off the national debt and related obligations. I have no idea whether $17 trillion is even close to the right amount. I know that even if the money dropped from heaven, you can't stroll into the bank with $17,000,000,000,000 in small bills and walk out a debt-free country. Sure, it's much more complicated than that. But it's not more complicated than D-day. And it's the least we can do.

8

AN ENCOUNTER IN THE STOCKROOM

Years ago, when I was the editor of *Harper's,* we employed a "mentally retarded" (as the term was back then) man named Joe as our "office boy" (as the term was back then). He sorted the mail, ran simple errands, and kept the stockroom stocked. One day I went to the stockroom in search of typing paper (as the term was back then), opened the supply cabinet, and stared at the contents but didn't see what I was looking for. Joe was there, and I asked him, "Hey Joe, are we out of typing paper?" He pointed to a ream at eye level. "Gosh," I said, "how in the world did I miss that?" Joe smiled sweetly and said, "Don't worry, Mike, it happens to me all the time."

ACKNOWLEDGMENTS

This book could not have been written without the help of a long list of skilled doctors who not only advised me on the book but also kept me alive and functioning at a reasonably high level for the past few years while I wrote it. So thanks to Dr. Leland Teng at the Virginia Mason Clinic in Seattle; Dr. Monique Giroux and physician's assistant Sierra Faris at any number of places, including the Cleveland Clinic; Dr. Ali Rezai, formerly of the Cleveland Clinic and now at Ohio State; Evergreen Hospital and the Booth Gardner Parkinson's Center in Kirkland, WA; Dr. Howard Hurtig, Dr. Matt Stern, and Dr. Kathy Lawler at the University of Pennsylvania; Dr. Ergun Uc at the University of Iowa; Dr. Mark Mapstone at the University of Rochester; Tim Quigley of the University of Washington (and my brother-in-law); and Dr. George Ricaurte and Dr. Paul Ladenson, among many others, at Johns Hopkins University.

ACKNOWLEDGMENTS

Some of the material in this book was published in a different version in *The New Yorker*. Thanks to all there, especially to Dorothy Wickenden. Thanks to all at *The Atlantic,* which published a version of the least entertaining chapter of this book—you can guess which one that is—especially James Gibney and James Bennett. And thanks to Graydon Carter and Cullen Murphy of *Vanity Fair* for . . . oh, where to start? But thanks.

This book is dedicated to Russell, Jasper, Matt, Crystal, Sandy, Neal, Susan, Patty, and Michael J. Fox.